Teacher Education for Transformative Agency

Critical perspectives on design, content and pedagogy

EDITORS
Carina America | Nazeem Edwards | Maureen Robinson

Teacher education for transformative agency: Critical perspectives on design, content and pedagogy

Published by African Sun Media under the SUN PReSS imprint

All rights reserved

Copyright © 2020 African Sun Media and the editors

This publication was subjected to an independent double-blind peer evaluation by the publisher.

The editors and the publisher have made every effort to obtain permission for and acknowledge the use of copyrighted material. Refer all enquiries to the publisher.

No part of this book may be reproduced or transmitted in any form or by any electronic, photographic or mechanical means, including photocopying and recording on record, tape or laser disk, on microfilm, via the Internet, by e-mail, or by any other information storage and retrieval system, without prior written permission by the publisher.

Views reflected in this publication are not necessarily those of the publisher.

First edition 2020

ISBN 978-1-928480-92-1
ISBN 978-1-928480-93-8 (e-book)
https://doi.org/10.18820/9781928480938

Set in Californian FB 11/14

Cover design, typesetting and production by African Sun Media

SUN PReSS is an imprint of African Sun Media. Scholarly, professional and reference works are published under this imprint in print and electronic formats.

This publication can be ordered from:
orders@africansunmedia.co.za
Takealot: bit.ly/2monsfl
Google Books: bit.ly/2k1Uilm
africansunmedia.store.it.si *(e-books)*
Amazon Kindle: amzn.to/2ktL.pkL

Visit africansunmedia.co.za for more information.

TABLE OF CONTENTS

01 Introduction: Purpose, outline and contribution of the book 1

Carina America, Nazeem Edwards & Maureen Robinson

SECTION A: Deliberations within core modules

02 Practical learning for ethical agency in teaching 13

Maureen Robinson

03 Teaching educational psychology: Creating an epistemological disposition 33

Karlien Conradie

04 Teaching a new generation: Implications for Curriculum Studies 53

Marie Louise Botha

05 Auto-ethnographic reflections on an Education Governance, Leadership and Management module 73

Jerome Joorst

06 Teacherly being and becoming on the PGCE programme: The early emergence of students' reflexive mediations of curriculum knowledge and pedagogy on the History and Sociology of Education module 101

Aslam Fataar & Jennifer Feldman

SECTION B: Deliberations within subject-specific modules

07 Teaching business ethics to pre-service teachers: An integrated approach ... 125

Carina America

08 Exploring pre-service science teachers' epistemic agency to develop their pedagogy for science teaching ... 145

Nazeem Edwards

SECTION C: Conclusion

09 An agenda for reinventing teacher education in South Africa: Next steps for deliberation ... 169

Marie Brennan

Contributors

Carina America is a Senior Lecturer in the Department of Curriculum Studies at Stellenbosch University's Faculty of Education. She is the coordinator of the Postgraduate Certificate in Education (PGCE) programme and has been involved in the recurriculation of the PGCE for Economics, Business Studies and Accounting. Over the past decade, she participated in several national research projects related to curriculum analysis, development, and assessment in Business Education.

Marie Louise Botha is a Senior Lecturer in the Department of Curriculum Studies at Stellenbosch University. She is a former coordinator of the B Ed and PGCE programmes, and served on both the re-curriculation committees during 2013-2015. Her areas of interest include curriculum inquiry, science teacher education, teaching and learning and mentorship. She has supervised and co-supervised MEd and PhD students successfully and has been an external examiner for numerous PhD and Masters degree theses.

Marie Brennan is based in Australia where she retired in 2016. She is Extraordinary Professor at Stellenbosch University and Adjunct Professor at the University of South Australia, where she had a term as Dean of Education and Honorary Professor at Victoria University, Melbourne. She remains active in research, supervision of doctoral students and community engagement. Recent publications focus on students as researchers; curriculum addressing social injustice, the 'anthropocene', indigenous and decoloniality; higher education, especially teacher education.

Karlien Conradie is a lecturer in the Department of Educational Psychology, Stellenbosch University. She is also an educational psychologist registered with the Health Professions Council of South Africa (HPCSA). Her research focuses on the onto-phenomenological ability and aesthetic disposition concerning both psychotherapy and teaching as well as how this can be stimulated in an often mechanistic and utilitarian environment.

Nazeem Edwards is a Senior Lecturer in the Department of Curriculum Studies at Stellenbosch University. He is a former coordinator of the Postgraduate Certificate in Education programme and served on its recurriculation committee since 2013. His research interests are within the broader field of Science Education, with a focus on the development of prospective science teachers' pedagogy in Chemistry and Physics at the high school level. He is actively involved as a research consultant with Umalusi.

Aslam Fataar is a Distinguished Professor in Sociology of Education at Stellenbosch University. He is a former president of the South African Education Research Association and Editor-in-Chief of the journal, *Southern African Review of Education*. He is currently seconded to a research and development chair position in the university's Transformation Office. Aslam has published three books, co-authored one book, and edited or co-edited six books.

Jennifer Feldman is a Lecturer in the Department of Education Policy Studies at Stellenbosch University. Before completing her PhD in 2016 she was a teacher and school principal in various school contexts. Her research is situated in the sociology of education and considers issues of education, policy and management, as well as topics relating to teaching and learning both in schools and higher education institutions.

Jerome Joorst is a lecturer in the Department of Education Policy Studies at Stellenbosch University. His research focus is in the areas of Sociology of Education and more specifically Rural Education. His research interests and publications are in teachers and learners' experiences and perspectives of the education system.

Maureen Robinson is a Professor in the Department of Curriculum Studies at Stellenbosch University. She has worked as a high school teacher in low-income schools, and a lecturer and materials developer at the University of the Western Cape, teaching action research and curriculum innovation. She has served as Dean of the Faculty of Education at the Cape Peninsula University of Technology (2002-2012) and Stellenbosch University (2012-2017). She has published widely in the areas of teacher education and educational reform and participated in national and international research and policy structures for teacher education.

Introduction: Purpose, outline and contribution of the book

Carina America, Nazeem Edwards & Maureen Robinson

Background and purpose of the book

One of the most important challenges in South Africa since the advent of democracy in 1994 has been to enhance the provision and quality of education for all. Yet while there has been much progress in increasing the number of young people attending school, stark systemic challenges and inadequate remedying of the apartheid legacies of separation and inequality remain pervasive (Christie, 2018).

A range of education policies have been introduced over the years in an attempt to address these concerns. Sayed, Carrim, Badroodien, McDonald and Singh (2018) outline in detail the development of these policies as they relate to teacher education. A contributing factor to policy re-development was the review of professional programmes in Education, undertaken in 2006 by the Higher Education Quality Committee (HEQC) of the Council on Higher Education (CHE). The report on this process described some key findings relating to initial teacher education programmes, one of which was weak programme design (CHE, 2010).[1] Following this process, the *Minimum Requirements for Teacher Education Qualifications* (MRTEQ) (DHET, 2011, revised 2015) was published as national policy to address the critical challenges that education in South Africa faced – especially the concerns about weak content and conceptual knowledge found amongst teachers.

MRTEQ identifies different types of knowledge that underpin teachers' practice and that need to be part of an initial teacher education programme. Five types of learning are identified and associated with the acquisition, integration and application of knowledge for teaching, namely: disciplinary, pedagogical, practical, fundamental and situational learning. Each of these learning types is explained in the policy, together with information about subject knowledge, pedagogical strategies, the world of practice, languages and information and communication technology (ICT), and the varied learning situations found in the country. The expectation is that teachers should be able to draw reflexively from these different forms of knowledge to work in an integrated and applied manner. The policy also emphasises the need for teachers to learn to work in ways that address the lingering effects of apartheid and to develop competences to deal with diversity, inclusivity and environmental sustainability. Professional ethics and the development of professional attitudes and values are also seen as key elements of teacher education.

The MRTEQ policy foregrounds knowledge, reflection, connection, synthesis and research in its conceptualisation of teacher educators' work. As such, it provides an overall structure for learning programmes at the same time as allowing for institutional flexibility and discretion in the final design. It encourages teacher educators to become engaged in communities of practice working towards curriculum design, policy implementation and research.

Against this policy background, a newly designed Postgraduate Certificate in Education (PGCE) was implemented in the Faculty of Education at Stellenbosch University in 2018. This gave lecturers the impetus for critical reflection on the purpose, structure and content of their modules, a process that led to the key question of this book, namely: How (can) do we prepare teachers for South Africa at this time?

---

1   The following terminology is used interchangeably in the book: teacher educators/lecturers; pre-service teachers/ student teachers. It should also be noted that primary and high school students are referred to as 'learners' in South Africa.

The book is the product of many months of deliberation and critical reflection by colleagues teaching on the PGCE programme. Workshops were held where lecturers could engage with the structure and conceptual framework of the programme as a whole, as well as of their particular module. This culminated in a symposium at the South African Education Research Association (SAERA) conference in Pretoria in 2018, as lecturers examined how curriculum design unfolds across disciplines in the programme, and crucially, the commonalities in the presentation of course material.

Each chapter in the book deals with theoretical frameworks that underpin the thinking and practices of these teacher educators. Using research-based and self-study methodologies, chapters include a description of the content and pedagogy of a particular module, its deeper educational purpose, conception of knowledge for teaching, and connection to the wider frame of educational transformation and social justice. In keeping with the reflexive exploration of their work, authors ask: How do I work with this in my practice? To answer this question, authors deliberate on the hopes, frustrations, complexities and dilemmas of their work, as they seek to enact particular educational goals in their teaching.

A number of key principles informed the process of deliberation. These included:

- How to navigate within teacher education from the ravages of apartheid education to inclusive, democratic practices that address the developmental needs of the majority of our citizens.
- The desire to move out of academic 'silos' and to work across subjects and departments to build a shared understanding of the programme.
- How to ensure structural and conceptual coherence across the programme, while allowing lecturers the academic freedom to engage students critically within their discipline.
- How to engage with the demands of knowledge-building in the twenty-first century
- How to integrate different forms of knowledge across the curriculum.

Two frames of reference were helpful in constructing the discourse. The first was that of Productive Pedagogies (Hayes, Mills, Christie & Lingard, 2006), with its four dimensions of intellectual quality, connectedness, a supportive classroom environment and working with and valuing difference. Second, the idea of Hordern (2018:787) that: "it is important to make the distinction between knowledge *about* education and knowledge *for* educational practice," was engaged with during discussions. As can be seen in the chapters, these frames of reference took on different shapes in the final module designs, with lecturers drawing to a greater or lesser extent on the key concepts of these theories.

An outline of the chapters

At Stellenbosch University the PGCE is a one-year full-time teaching qualification that follows on from an undergraduate degree, and which is aimed at prospective high school teachers. Students register for eight compulsory generic subjects, and one or two teaching specialisation subjects. They spend about eight weeks on school-based observation and practice.

The book follows the logic of the programme structure and is divided into three sections. **Section A** focuses on a selection of the generic modules in the PGCE, or those compulsory modules that every student follows. **Section B** is devoted to a selection of subject-specific modules, the choice of which is dependent on the school subjects that the student intends to teach. **Section C** is the only chapter not written by a full-time member of staff at Stellenbosch University; it has the purpose of reflecting on broader historical, political and pedagogical issues emerging from the book and identifying further work that needs to be done.

In the first chapter of Section A, Maureen Robinson draws on the notion of educational virtuosity to discuss **Practical Learning,** a module that includes both university-based lectures and school placements. While the immediate aim of this module is to advance student teacher professional learning, it has the more fundamental purpose of embedding practical tools for classroom practice within situated judgement and ethical agency, and within an understanding of social forces. The chapter describes the design and pedagogy of the module, and reports on research into students' experiences of their preparation for a diversity of learners and a range of social contexts. The chapter then considers if and how the lectures and the school observation impacted on students' own sense of agency within the diverse and unequal contexts of South African schools.

Karlien Conradie maps some of the central and linking aspects underlying the learning relationship in her module, **Psychology of Education**. These include emotional security (trust), healthy psychological boundaries, interconnectedness, individuation and attachment security. She argues that a caring, receptive disposition starts from the premise that humans are inherently relational, responsive beings. She sees the human condition as one of connectedness and interdependence where people experience themselves in relation to others, but individual psychological and social boundaries are not dismissed. Having described in detail the rationale for the module, Conradie explains how on its completion, teacher students should have critical insight into the developmental dimensions of adolescence. The interaction between development and the learning process is explored here together with discussion of influences on teaching practice, including effective mediation and support of diverse learning abilities.

Marie Louise Botha uses the lens of the module **Curriculum Studies** to revisit teaching and learning (curriculum) in teacher education, and to ask what is in store for the twenty-first century. Based on her experience of students struggling to critically engage with content, she looks at the curriculum of the module to determine its alignment with the demands and needs of the 'new generation' student cohort. She links this self-reflection to the goal of promoting engaged and informed citizen-teachers who are able to contribute positively within the unpredictable future of a global pandemic, economic inequality and environmental challenges.

Jerome Joorst's purpose is to reflect on the content and possible outcomes of the module **Education Governance, Leadership and Management**. Following an auto-ethnographical methodology, he asks what can be learnt from the pedagogical design of the module in terms of preparing students for the realities of teaching. Joorst argues that the demands of what good teachers should look like, coupled with complexities in the histories and current education realities of the country, with its continuing two-tiered and unequal education system, places heavy demands on teacher education. He outlines the daily, lived experience of being a teacher educator in South Africa, including within the university's institutional culture, what is expected to be taught in the module, the identities of the students and how non-traditional academics in the university do their teaching. He then elaborates on three emerging challenges in his work, namely working in a regulative environment, knowing who we teach and how they learn, and deciding what knowledge to include in the course. In so doing, Joorst is able to become conscious of how his students engage with the module, and also how he views himself in relation to his teaching.

In the final chapter in Section A, Aslam Fataar and Jennifer Feldman reflect on the module **History and Sociology of Education**, arguing that learning to become a professional teacher involves not only what the students are learning, but also who they are and who they are becoming. The authors discuss an assignment where students were asked to draw on the module's readings and class and tutorial discussions to consider how the life trajectories of students with different histories had positioned them in their 'becoming' as student teachers. The key argument of the chapter is that students' reflexive engagement with the module readings and discussions in relation to their own biographies supported the potential for them to begin to shift how they think about themselves in relation to their emerging 'teacherly' identity. Through this process, secondary habitus layers were being formed that have the potential to impact and change who students are becoming as pre-service teachers within the South African educational context.

Section B focuses on two subject-specific curricula within the PGCE programme. In the first, Carina America reflects on the notion of business ethics in the subject **Business Studies Teaching**. She asks the question if, and the extent to which, pre-service business teachers should be pro-active in their teaching about moral right and wrong that govern business or organisational decision-making. Using a self-study approach, she explores the integration of business ethics for pre-service business teachers within the Productive Pedagogies framework, focusing on the aspects of substantive conversation and knowledge as problematic. Her argument is that excellence in the business world presupposes a broad education that includes ethical integrity and virtuous behaviour in a business environment. Business Studies teacher educators, however, are often not critical about the capacity of the formal curriculum to mediate learning that raises questions about the conduct and decision-making of corporate businesses. Practical issues are highlighted to illustrate the importance of ethical sensitivity in the Business Studies Teaching module.

Focusing on **Science Education**, Nazeem Edwards argues that his role as a teacher educator is to develop prospective science teachers as epistemic agents in the classroom. He discusses the challenge of teaching graduates in Physics and Chemistry to recontextualise their disciplinary knowledge for the purposes of teaching. His argument is that the prospective science teacher needs pedagogical knowledge for teaching which brings together the disciplinary discourses and educational research that relates to pedagogy. He outlines his use of multiple representations as a pedagogical approach to mediate scientific knowledge. Drawing on examples of students' own classroom practice, he shows the challenges of shifting the epistemic agency of his students. Examples are provided of students who promote science as an accumulation of knowledge or as an established body of knowledge, or who have a conservative teaching approach that holds onto cognitive authority within the classroom.

Section C was written by Marie Brennan, who acted as a critical friend during the process of writing this book. Brennan is an Extraordinary Professor in the Faculty of Education at Stellenbosch University, and has visited regularly from Australia to work with staff and students. She is also an adjunct professor at the University of South Australia, where she was a Dean of Education. Her work in teacher education is well known internationally and she has been active in both pedagogical research and policy analysis around curriculum for addressing educational inequality. In this chapter, she offers a problematisation about both education and teacher education's positioning in South Africa at this time. Most importantly, she challenges us all to deepen the conversation about the next phases of scholarship and practice that might emerge from the deliberations raised in these chapters.

Intended contribution

Darling-Hammond (2006) has argued that successful teacher education programmes include careful sequencing, a strong theory of learning to teach and an intersection of subjects, aggregated into a well-understood landscape of learning. At the same time, she cautions that: "… creating coherence has been difficult in teacher education because of departmental divides [and] individualistic norms" (2006:306). As a counter to the individualistic norms referred to here, the book at its very least documents an attempt to work collaboratively and productively across subjects and departments, and to share conceptual frameworks and practical teaching moments.

The second contribution of this book, we believe, is to provide insight into and respect for teacher education as academic work (Ellis & McNicholl, 2015). Green, Reid and Brennan (2017) have argued that teacher education is "struggling to thrive as an intellectual and practical endeavour in a policy context that increasingly seeks to render it as an instrumental field" (2017:39). Thus, while policymakers and politicians might at times simplify what it takes to prepare teachers for the nation, the chapters here illustrate the complexity of the task, showing how biography, policy, research, theory and practice intersect in the daily work of teacher education. The chapters also illustrate the multi-faceted (and contestable) nature of 'knowledge for teaching', thereby opening up avenues for ongoing debate and discussion.

There are many more questions to be addressed than have been raised in this book; we are fortunate that some of these are highlighted in the concluding chapter. The chapters are, to some extent, inward-looking, providing a window into how teacher educators in a particular place and time are grappling with their intentions and actions. Follow-up studies would be needed to ascertain any longer-term influence on student teachers' enacted professional vision and practices.

High expectations exist in South Africa for education to make a difference to the life chances of all young people, and teacher education is not released from this responsibility. Student protests in 2015 and 2016 in the #FeesMustFall and #RhodesMustFall campaigns have thrown calls for transformation in our social system into sharp relief, including focusing on the ideological and material role of education in maintaining South Africa's highly inequitable society. Indeed the imperative to address the endemic challenges of a post-apartheid education system means that: "teacher [educator] voice cannot be simply about assertion of individualistic goals, but extensions of a social and collective reconstructivist responsibility" (Samuel, 2014:619).

Like others around the world, we believe that learning to be a teacher is not just about qualification and socialisation, but also about consideration of what is educationally desirable (Biesta, 2015). We hope that, in some small way, this book may make a contribution to this purpose.

References

Biesta, G.J.J. 2015. How does a competent teacher become a good teacher? On judgement, wisdom and virtuosity in teaching and teacher education. In: R. Heilbronn & L. Foreman-Peck (eds), *Philosophical perspectives on teacher education*. Chichester: Wiley-Blackwell, pp. 3-22. https://doi.org/10.1002/9781118977859.ch1

Christie, P. 2018. Foreword. In: Y. Sayed, N. Carrim, A. Badroodien, Z. McDonald & M. Singh (eds), *Learning to teach in post-apartheid South Africa: Student teachers' encounters with initial teacher education*. Stellenbosch: African Sun Media, pp. xxiii-xxvi.

CHE (Council on Higher Education). 2010. *Report on the national review of academic and professional programmes in education*. Cape Town: Jacana Media.

Darling-Hammond, L. 2006. Constructing 21st-century teacher education. *Journal of Teacher Education*, 57(3):300-314. https://doi.org/10.1177/0022487105285962

DHET (Department of Higher Education and Training). 2011. The *Minimum Requirements for Teacher Education Qualifications*. Government Gazette No 34467. Pretoria, South Africa: Department of Higher Education and Training.

DHET (Department of Higher Education and Training). 2015. *Revised policy on the minimum requirements for teacher education qualifications*. Government Gazette No 38487. Pretoria, South Africa: Department of Higher Education and Training.

Ellis, V. & McNicholl, J. 2015. *Transforming teacher education: Reconfiguring the academic work*. London and New York: Bloomsbury.

Green, B., Reid, J.A. & Brennan, M. 2017. Challenging policy, rethinking practice: struggling for the soul of teacher education. In: T. Trippestad, A. Swennen & T. Werler (eds), *The struggle for teacher education: International perspectives on governance and reform*. London and New York: Bloomsbury, pp. 39-55. https://doi.org/10.5040/9781474285568.0008

Hayes, D., Mills, M., Christie, P. & Lingard, B. 2006. *Teachers and schooling making a difference: Productive pedagogies, assessment and performance*. Crows Nest: Allen & Unwin.

Hordern, J. 2018. Is powerful educational knowledge possible? *Cambridge Journal of Education*, 48(6):787-802.

Samuel, M. 2014. South African teacher voices: Recurring resistances and reconstructions for teacher education and development. *Journal of Education for Teaching*, 40(5):610-621.

Sayed, Y., Carrim, N., Badroodien, A., McDonald, Z. & Singh, M. 2018. Policy and legislative context of initial teacher education in South Africa. In: Y. Sayed, N. Carrim, A. Badroodien, Z. McDonald & M. Singh (eds), *Learning to teach in post-apartheid South Africa: Student teachers' encounters with initial teacher education*. Stellenbosch: African Sun Media, pp. 27-40. https://doi.org/10.18820/9781928357971

SECTION A
Deliberations within core modules

Practical learning for ethical agency in teaching

Maureen Robinson

Introduction

Around the world, teacher education programmes expect that their pre-service teachers undertake some practical orientation, usually, but not exclusively, in the form of a placement in a school. This chapter reflects on a module entitled Practical Learning within the one-year Postgraduate Certificate in Education (PGCE) at Stellenbosch University. In a country like South Africa, with its high levels of racial, educational and social inequality, there is an imperative to design teacher education within a framework of social justice. Following from this imperative, the immediate aim of this module is to advance student teacher professional learning. More fundamentally, however, the module seeks to embed practical tools for classroom practice within the deeper purposes of situated judgement and ethical agency. Through lectures, school observations and teaching opportunities, student teachers are exposed to teaching and learning methods, and opportunities to promote their own growth, theorise practice and become confident, competent teachers. Students are encouraged to recognise the complexity of teaching and to debate key concepts and practices of teaching, thus advancing the notion of a critical and reflective practitioner.

The module is underpinned by the notion of educational virtuosity (Biesta, 2015). Biesta argues that the teaching of knowledge and skills, or socialisation into the community of teachers, may bring about teachers who are competent; however, such teachers "may lack the embodied ability to place their knowledge, skills and ways of doing within the wider context of the question of what is to be done, the question of what is educationally desirable" (Biesta, 2015:19). With this in mind, the module follows principles for fostering teacher agency within an understanding of social forces. This purpose is explicitly communicated to students with a message that the module (and the PGCE programme in general) is intended "to prepare South African teachers for South African schools". This implies a commitment to working within, and for, the wide diversity of social and educational contexts in the country, with a view to improving the educational (and life) chances of all.

The chapter begins by describing the design of the module. It then focuses on two areas of interest. First, I outline the conceptual and pedagogical considerations that formed the background to the theory lectures. Second, I report on research into students' experiences of the module, as contained in their reflections during school observation, as well as interviews about the module's contribution to their preparation for a diversity of contexts. Drawing on the notion of 'embodiment' (Ord & Nuttall, 2016), the purpose of the chapter is to consider if and how the lectures and school observation impacted on students' own sense of agency within the diverse and unequal contexts of South African schools.

The design of the module

The module runs from February to November. It is a compulsory element of the PGCE and forms almost 25% of the programme credits. It consists of five components, namely:
- two weeks of observation in a school prior to the start of the university academic year,
- one or two days of observation in local schools,
- weekly microteaching and lesson analysis of peers,
- a school-based practicum of ten consecutive weeks in the third term of the year, and
- eighteen weeks of lectures prior to, and following on from, the school practicum.

The combination of these components, together with the student's particular curriculum specialisation, is intended to provide an integrated experience of learning from and in practice. This experience is described in South African policy as follows:

> Learning from practice includes the study of practice, using discursive resources to analyse different practices across a variety of contexts, drawing from case studies, video records, lesson observations, etc., in order to theorise practice and form a basis for learning in practice. Learning in practice involves teaching in authentic and simulated classroom environments. (DHET, 2015:10)

Figure 2.1 provides a visual representation of the different components and their specific purposes. In 2018, the year in which this research was conducted, there were about 240 students in the class. The student body has become more diverse over the years with a noteworthy mix of gender, age, race, prior work experience and political leanings in the class.

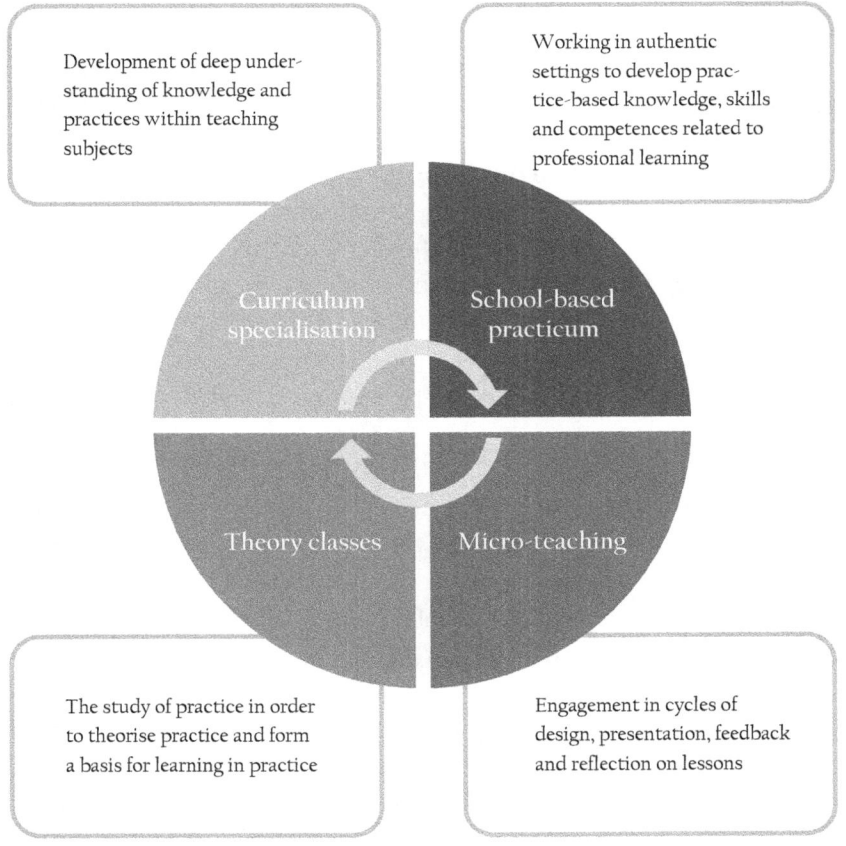

Figure 2.1 Practical learning: learning from, in and for practice

National and institutional policies

The purpose and design of the module links directly to national policy imperatives in teacher education, as well as to institutional frameworks of Stellenbosch University.

'Situational learning' is one of the principles underpinning teacher education policy in South Africa, as stated in the revised *Minimum Requirements for Teacher Education Qualifications* (DHET, 2015). This refers to the need for new teachers to know about varied learning situations, contexts and environments of education and be able to "draw reflexively from integrated and applied knowledge, so as to work flexibly and effectively in a variety of contexts" (DHET, 2015:9).

At an institutional level, Stellenbosch University has committed to a set of graduate attributes (Stellenbosch University: Strategy for teaching and learning 2017–2021). The purpose and design of the Practical Learning module reflects a number of these intended attributes. These include an enquiring mind, exercising responsibility for learning and using knowledge, an engaged citizen, critical and creative thinking, and being effective in a diverse environment. Such attributes are pursued in the module through creating opportunities for student teachers to recognise the complexity of teaching, debate key concepts and practices of teaching, and develop personal and professional agency. The notion of an engaged citizen resonates further with the commitment expressed by the Faculty of Education to expand students' insights and experiences, through actively encouraging them to move out of their comfort zones during the school-based components of their programme.

Pedagogical principles

Policy and institutional imperatives can be distilled into a number of pedagogical principles that underpin the design and content of the module. These include:
- Connecting the theory and practice of teaching.
- Supporting professional practice and professional becoming.
- Advancing knowledge, skills and dispositions for teaching.
- Critical reflection and ethical agency.

The module Practical Learning draws on a number of theoretical categories in its conceptualisation and design. The notion of educational virtuosity (Biesta, 2015) has already been mentioned. Other influences on the approach to the module include the link between emotions, identity and subjectivity

(Zembylas, 2003), practice architecture (Kemmis, 2018), teacher education and social justice (Zeichner, 2009), the soul of teacher education (Green et al., 2017) and situational judgement and moral responsibility (Winch, 2017). In combination, these theorists build a picture of teacher education that seeks to develop novice teachers as ethical, critical and responsible agents, working in grounded ways within particular social and institutional frameworks towards better educational and life chances for all.

Translated into classroom (or, in this instance, lecture hall) practice, the module is characterised by an approach to teaching and learning that foregrounds educational dilemmas, authentic scenarios, a problem-posing rather than a recipe-understanding of the work of the teacher, and active engagement on the part of students (even with a class of over 200 students). Pedagogical approaches are built around linking cognition, affect and agency, connecting concepts and contexts, and promoting a commitment to democracy, diversity and citizenship. Curriculum materials that integrate these approaches in concrete ways include questions to students on, for example, which forms of knowledge for teaching they feel confident (or not confident) about, and how they might address this, as well as structured observation tasks that encourage students to reflect on the relationship between schools and society.

Acknowledging the contested nature of the knowledge base for teaching (Winch, 2017), the nature of the module is such that there is no obvious body of academic content. Topics include Shulman's knowledge for teaching (2004), Productive Pedagogies (Gore et al., 2004), the teacher as a mediator of learning, the use of media, lesson planning, classroom management, reflecting on teaching, professional standards for teaching, and the rights and responsibilities of teaching. As can be seen, the lecture topics work within a combination of different domains of learning to be a teacher. These include 'formal knowledge' (e.g. learning about conceptions of knowledge for teaching), 'everyday' knowledge (exposure to the experiences of teachers), technological skills for teaching (e.g. digital pedagogy), and issues related to socio-epistemic forces and the requirements of professional practice (e.g. school cultures, policy frameworks) (see Hordern, 2018, for a discussion of the relationship between different forms of educational knowledge).

Each of these domains of learning has thrown up its own set of dilemmas for myself as the lecturer in selecting curriculum materials. For example, which 'knowledges for teaching' are most powerful in teaching students in a relatively compressed period to become 'good' teachers? What modes of classroom practice are appropriate in what situations and for what purposes? To what extent should the module engage with students' biographies and values in its attempt to promote personal agency? Should new teachers study policy and regulatory frameworks from a perspective of critique, or a perspective that tends towards compliance, and probable successful assimilation into the culture of the school?

The movement across domains of learning becomes particularly noticeable as the module progresses into the third term of the academic year and students ready themselves for the school-based practicum. As students traverse the boundaries of the different activity systems of school and university (Max, 2010), their challenge becomes to bridge these sites of learning in ways that are mutually meaningful for themselves as student teachers, the teachers, and the learners at school.

Many tensions are pertinent here. Students are now expected to move from an emphasis on critical reflection to the demonstration of skills and competences. They are no longer outsiders to the school, but (semi) insiders with all the related expectations. Their approach to learning moves from abstraction of knowledge to action and implementation. Policy critique must become policy compliance if they are to 'market' themselves for a job at that school once they graduate. They are no longer individuals accountable only to themselves, but members of a much bigger community. And, on a very immediate level, they have to face new practical considerations of travel time, punctuality, dress code and – in many instances – anxiety about personal safety in difficult social conditions.

Against this background, the task of the teacher educator becomes particularly complex. Unlike many other university-based degrees, a professional programme like teacher education goes beyond teaching concepts 'for the mind'. Rather, it must teach others to enter the world of practice within frames of professional competence and a set of values. The module must move beyond the (usually futile) attempt to bridge theory and practice, and rather find ways of building knowledge for teaching that is "integrated and embodied, rather than in consciously cognitive terms" (Ord & Nuttall, 2016:355).

This challenge leads me to the second part of the chapter. Having conceptualised the Practical Learning module against a set of principles, questions arose around curriculum implementation. Here again, a set of dilemmas arise for the lecturer: What is the conceptual and practical 'toolbox' for ethical agency? How to make concepts and practices part of student teachers' own repertoire of thinking and classroom practice? How to combine knowledge, skills and dispositions towards a democratic purpose? How to combine the cognitive and affective domains of teaching in order to remain motivated and committed to good teaching? Questions like these led to a decision to explore aspects of students' own experiences of the module.

Exploring student teachers' perspectives

In this second part of the chapter, I report on a research project which set out to investigate how student teachers articulated their experiences of the module's aim to embed tools for classroom practice within the deeper purpose of ethical agency.

The research approach can be located within design-based research. Amongst other purposes, design-based research looks to explore possibilities for new learning and teaching environments and to develop theories of learning and instruction that are contextually-based (Herrington & Reeves, 2011). Having identified a 'problem' in my teaching (How best to connect purpose and pedagogy in teacher education?), I set out to research students' experiences of these pedagogical principles, with a view to improving the module and identifying further principles around teacher education for ethical agency. Methods of data gathering were:

- tracking the schools student teachers choose for their observations and school placements, and their reasons for choosing these schools. Analysis focused on the extent to which these schools differed from students' own educational backgrounds;
- guided reflection tasks from the first school observation;
- focus group interviews to explore which concepts, theories or approaches in the module or programme influenced students' thinking or teaching.

The chapter reports only on the findings of the last two points, as this is where the most robust evidence was obtained.

The first school observation reports were constructed as guided questions, aimed at leading students to work in authentic settings (the classroom) to identify examples of practice that illustrated Productive Pedagogies, prior to them being exposed to any theory. Thus, rather than asking students to identify the concepts of intellectual quality, supportive environment, recognition of difference, and connectedness (Gore et al., 2014), they were asked to describe their observations of, for example, confirmation that learners understood the content of the lesson, or classroom management that supports learning.

In line with the goal of learning to work flexibly in a variety of contexts, the school observation included the following instruction to students: "Students are strongly encouraged to select a school that is different from the school they attended as a learner. Examples of differences could be: socio-economic, racial, cultural or religious background of the learners, language of instruction, urban/rural, etc."

The focus group interviews were arranged later in the year. In October 2018 an invitation was extended to the whole class to be part of a discussion "to explore if and how the PGCE programme, in particular the module Practical Learning, has influenced students' thinking about being a teacher in the diversity of schooling and social contexts in South Africa." Fourteen students responded positively; they were divided into four focus groups of three to four students each and interviewed by a research assistant using a set of questions for about an hour per group.

The nature of the sampling process meant that the demographic backgrounds of the interviewees were not fully reflective of the class composition as a whole, although the group was diverse in many ways. Table 2.1 provides a summary of the student teachers who were interviewed. Ethical procedures included institutional permission to conduct the research, signed informed consent forms by all students and the assurance that all identifying information would be kept confidential.

Table 2.1 Overview of the pre-service teachers interviewed for this study

Gender	Male - 2			Female - 12			
Race	African	2	Coloured	1	White	9	Not indicated	2
Home language	Afrikaans	5	English	8	Setswana	1	Sesotho	1
Teaching subjects	English, Life Orientation, Accounting, Mathematical Literacy, Life Sciences, Business Studies, Afrikaans, Geography, History, Mathematics, isiXhosa						

Findings from the school observation reports

The responses analysed here were given as answers to the following question in the observation reports: What did I learn about schooling in South Africa? Students were asked to describe briefly (1–2 paragraphs each) examples observed in terms of:

- Impact of socio-economic factors on teaching and learning.
- Positive approaches to managing diversity (e.g. language, race, gender, religion, ability, etc.).
- How a school can contribute to building a democratic society.

Due to the volume of data contained in over 200 school observation reports, as well as the richness of the responses, it was decided to focus the analysis on the first and third questions only.

Impact of socio-economic factors on teaching and learning

Even within the short two-week period that they were in schools, and prior to any exposure to an education qualification, PGCE students were well able to identify how socio-economic factors impact on teaching and learning. The data showed two main areas in which this was observed: at the school itself, and from the perspective of the community in which the school was located.

At the level of the school, students identified clear differences in facilities and opportunities available to learners in different socio-economic circumstances. They noted that at better resourced schools and in more affluent communities, learners had access to more subject choices (thus greater career options), more extramural opportunities (thus more opportunity for well-rounded development), more regular exposure to the Internet and better resources for teaching and learning (thus easier access to information), more excursions (thus greater opportunity for expanded experiences), and the more likely presence of school-based support units, like a school psychologist. Quotes from two students give a taste of their observation of the impact of socio-economic factors on teaching and learning:

> Many of the learners struggle to afford the books that are required by subjects [...] In terms of learning, it inhibits the choices some learners can make with regards to subjects, and also causes them to lag behind with classwork and homework. This affects the classroom, as the teacher must attempt to distribute books between every pair in order to allow for work to continue.

> Many learners experience a lack of access to educational resources at home, such as books and the Internet. This increases the amount of learning that must happen in the classroom, and often teachers must put more effort into assisting learners.

Wealthier parents could pay for additional teachers so that classes were smaller, and they had greater capacity for fundraising for additional equipment and resources. This advantage played out in academic achievement where success rates were higher and access to further studies (and better career options) more likely. In contrast, as one student explained:

> Because of the high rate of failure in the Grade 10 class the classes of the Grade 10s are extremely full. There is almost no place for the learners to sit. This causes a challenge for learners to learn. The teacher also finds it difficult to teach in such a cramped-up class because there is always a group disrupting the class.

From a community perspective, there were again observations about the differences and inequalities of opportunity for young learners. Parental involvement in the school was more present with more socially mobile families, as was additional learning support in the form of private tutors and extra lessons. Even where poorer schools offered extra lessons, learners were hampered in attending. As one student noted: "There are teachers that offer extra classes on Saturdays but due to lack of transport most of the students that do need help cannot make it."

Social factors such as crime in the community and gang violence stood out as impacting greatly on learners' capacities for effective study. The poor and unreliable state of public transport was a particular negative influence:

> Due to cable theft, trains are therefore delayed or cancelled. Busses and taxis are jam-packed due to the high influx of commuters using these modes of transport. This has a negative impact on teaching and learning. Classes start at 8.00 a.m. Learners arrive at 9.00 a.m., missing an hour of the lesson (if it is a double period) which also impacts on learners being on time delaying the progress of the lesson, i.e. the educator needs to update learners who are late.

In the midst of these difficulties, students noted the resilience of many schools as they worked to address the challenges:

> I have been so moved at the compassion, empathy and enthusiasm of the school, at how they are constantly thinking of new ways as to how they can contribute to society and the needy, when there are even people attending the school who also are in need of financial assistance themselves.

A number of students commented on the feeding schemes at many schools, the clothing banks, and even monthly donations from teachers to provide food for learners from low income households.

How a school can contribute to a democratic society

Again, within the short space of time that they were at the schools, student teachers could identify a range of ways in which schools could – and did – contribute to building a democratic society. They saw numerous examples of interventions within the structure and culture of the schools. These included classroom and school rules based on democratic participation, values and principles aimed at promoting a culture of respect, and codes of conduct based on accountability and responsibility. As one example:

> Firstly, the school has a complete transparency approach. Nothing is done in secret. Anything the learners want to know they have access to, and can ask about, for example, award criteria, or sports team selection. This encourages learners to understand how democracy works, in that things are supposed to be transparent and only for the good of the people.

A number of practices were also seen as examples of building democracy in action. For example:

> All pupils are given responsibilities in matric (Grade 12, the final year of basic education in South Africa). Each learner must take part in one or more school club or group. Matrics must organise and lead assembly meetings. All school learners were involved in neighbouring welfare organisations and helping nearby poor communities.

Bodies like the School Governing Body, Representative Council of Learners and prefects were seen as structures for the active participation of different constituencies, through discussion, planning and voting. Examples were observed of how certain teachers' practices modelled the building of democracy by promoting dialogues around contemporary issues and encouraging critical and intellectual engagement with subject content. School newspapers and discussion groups created forums for engagement and debate, a particularly impressive example being:

> Senior learners formed a student unity committee and organised meetings where they could discuss issues relating to race, gender or sexual orientation. All learners were encouraged to attend, as well as participate. It was a safe space where the purpose was to encourage sharing views that were not often heard or understood. This allowed the learners to take part in discussions on their own terms which would lead to better understanding of important social issues. It empowered learners to voice their views, opinions or concerns. It gave their peers an opportunity to understand, discuss or rebut these views and opinions.

While none of these findings are surprising, the significance of the observations lies in the way in which students were able to develop a mindset around the relationship between schools and society, and their potential place within this, prior to beginning their formal studies. Writing about a similar intervention at a different university in South Africa some years ago, Amin and Ramrathan (2009) refer to this as reframing memory, disrupting experience, destabilising learning and reconstructing uncertainty. Such processes, in combination, offer a way into self-reflection and sensitivity to context, essential elements of being a teacher in any setting. In the longer term, habits of reflection and inquiry about schools in context may contribute to professional communities that engage with educational issues in the interests of social justice (see Cochran-Smith, 2004).

Findings from the focus group interviews

This section of the chapter reports on responses in the focus group interviews to the following questions:

- Which school did you select for your first observation/school practicum? Is this school different from the high school/s you yourself attended? In what way? Why did you select this school?
- Many South African schools include a diversity of learners (race, language, religion, ability, etc). Do you think your PGCE has prepared you for teaching in a classroom characterised by diversity? Why do you say this? Which modules/ topics/theories/ approaches (if any) in the PGCE/Practical Learning module have been valuable in this regard? Why do you say this?
- South African schools are characterised by a diversity of social and educational contexts (socio-economic conditions, urban, rural etc.). Do you think your PGCE has prepared you to teach in a range of schooling contexts? Why do you say this? Which modules/topics/theories/approaches (if any) in the PGCE/ Practical Learning module have been valuable in this regard? Why do you say this?

Selection of schools for first observation and practicum

Students in the focus groups indicated a relatively even divide between those who chose schools that were different from the one they had attended, and those that were similar. For those who chose schools similar to their own, reasons were in every case due to convenience: "It was practical for me – we only have one school in our town and my sister teaches there so I went there". Transport costs played a big role too, with students not being able to travel easily beyond their own homes. This practical issue has been found in other cases to serve as a significant barrier when trying to expose students to different social contexts (Robinson, 2014). Poor public transport, heavy morning traffic and no student stipends, sadly and invariably seem to preclude the potential for students to experience the life of a community outside of their own neighbourhoods. This systemic challenge starkly illustrates the intertwining of educational and social factors, and the complexity of meeting the policy goal of situational and contextual learning.

It was interesting to note the conception of 'difference' for those who chose schools different from the one they had attended. While I had expected these differences to be understood primarily in racial or socio-economic terms, students were less focused on race and class, and added a wider range of features of 'difference': gender (single sex or co-educational), size of the school, religion, availability of particular school subjects and nature of school (e.g. an agricultural school, a school for orphans, a school with private sponsors or rural location). In all cases they explained their motivation as an opportunity for growth and challenge. Some wanted to expand their own experiences of South African society: "You hear all these prejudices. [I] thought it couldn't be that bad." "I wanted to go where I could have exposure to isiXhosa." Others focused on personal development: "I wanted something completely different – who wants to go back to where you went before?" One student saw this as a moment to challenge herself professionally:

> I went around in the area where I stay. I wanted the worst school that I can (find). I wanted a ghetto school; a school where there was gangsterism. I thought if I can survive in that type of school I can survive anywhere.

For others, there was a longer-term goal of personal growth:

> Before entering PGCE you don't know the value of going somewhere different, of entering unfamiliar terrain. You think, oh well, just go with the easiest, stay in the comfort zone. But during the PGCE the lecturers make you aware that you grow as a person when you enter unfamiliar terrain and when you are exposed to situations that you are not used to.

Even though students were strongly encouraged to go to different kinds of schools for their observation and their practicum, it was interesting to note that those who chose the same school, did so thoughtfully and deliberately: "I wanted to see how the learners had developed, how things had changed from the beginning of the year"; "I was more aware of things when I went back"; "The principal is inspirational".

Preparation to teach a diversity of learners and in a range of social contexts

Due to the overlap in responses, the two interview questions around a diversity of learners and a range of social contexts have been combined here.

The interviews rendered many positive examples of where students felt the PGCE had prepared them to teach a diverse range of learners and in a range of social contexts. The subjects History, Sociology, Philosophy and Psychology were indicated as most significant here. Relevant topics mentioned included inclusive education, difference and diversity, links between children's home and school lives, language across the curriculum, bias, psychological safety and self-esteem.

Pedagogically, they felt that a number of subjects in the PGCE encouraged debates and critical discussion, and showed them that teaching is "not a set formula that you can be provided with." In the Practical Learning module itself, the videos in the series *"Schools that Work"* (https://bit.ly/3paiChI) were overwhelmingly named as most significant. These videos show schools that are succeeding against the odds. As one student put it: "The videos showed that the area is very rural and the schools can still function and the kids are doing well. Makes you think – even if you have the worst you can still do well." This perspective was echoed by another student:

> [The videos] taught me that no matter how many students you have, if you approach education with a positive mindset, you can still teach them. Being able to see this in practice in the videos ... Children were sitting on the floor, but I could see that they still received a good education because the teacher had a passion for teaching.

A surprising addition here was the topic of digital learning, with one student linking this to the presence of different language groups in a school: "[Digital pedagogy] bridged the diversity in the class as I could visually show the learners the topics, bridge language gaps." For another student teacher, the PGCE as a whole provided an integrated experience in preparing him for a diversity of situations:

> Life Sciences taught me to teach in a context where learners have no resources – to use objects from daily life. (This) really helped me to realise what I have and what I don't have, and to find an alternative. It helped me to adapt my lessons to a different environment. Life Orientation – you learn to know your children, regardless of any economic environment; know what the child is going through, the child has the potential to grow. It's not about physical resources, but how you approach teaching. Education Management and Leadership – it is knowing where you are responsible for the children, emotional responsibility. (I learnt) a little bit through every module. Practical Learning integrated everything.

Many responses were, however, less positive. School placements for the practicum received some criticism, with students noting a bias towards placement in more privileged schools:

> In theory it has given us the foundation, the knowledge that there is diversity in classrooms, you need to acknowledge [...] Unfortunately, being in Stellenbosch, many of the students went to schools that are still in the bubble of more privileged schools. It does not prepare us for the reality of what is going on in the education system. Too many of the students were placed in those schools.

Similarly:

> To a certain extent I feel like the PGCE aimed to do that (prepare for diverse contexts). I don't feel like it succeeded in all aspects to be honest. Because I only attended privileged schools. It would be nice to have more exposure to schools where kids have other things to worry about than being on their cellphones.

Rather than criticising the programme, one student acknowledged the responsibility that he too might have had in selecting a particular school for his placement:

> In theory it has given us an understanding of what to do, an understanding of why certain learners have certain knowledge and understanding. In theory it has shown us that you have urban and rural schools and communities. In practice it hasn't necessarily shown all of us. Unless you made a decision to be placed in a different socio-economic context (many students stayed in their comfort zones). It has to do with personal attitude and your take on moving out of your own comfort zone.

Rural schooling was also seen to be neglected: "[The PGCE] did not prepare us for the *platteland* [rural areas] and their communities. It focused a lot on local schools: don't think about over the mountain. I don't want to live in the city." "A lot of our classes focus on digital learning, which is good. But they did not give us the tools on how to teach in a rural school where [there] could be no technology."

Lecturers' own distance from the experience of schooling was also noted as an obstacle to grappling with contemporary issues: "Most lecturers have been out of the class for a very long time and things have changed, and it is almost as if the theories they have are based on old observations." Those who had authentic cases to draw on were valued: "He would give us scenarios and he would tell us what he did and how he approached it, and that would help."

The overall message was an acknowledgement that the content and the pedagogy of the PGCE classes had been oriented towards preparing students for a diversity of contexts, and that students were definitely aware and sensitive to the issues. However, despite this movement in the direction of "ethical commitment and personal development ... as part of their occupational make-up" (Winch, 2017:15), students indicated that they did not feel prepared in a practical sense. One student summarised this as follows:

> There was an attempt – subjects taught us the theory to understand disadvantage. But I say the theory, because I don't think it practically prepared me to teach in those contexts. I am talking about my teaching subjects, e.g. I asked my lecturer about teaching where there were no resources. She sent an email with a few examples of resources. She didn't even know how to help us.

Overall findings

Attempting to design a module linked to Biesta's "educational virtuosity" (2015:19), the findings of the study demonstrate the many factors that can undermine or at least challenge such efforts. From the interviews in particular, it became clear that the module Practical Learning was but one relatively small element of the overall student experience, with a number of aspects of the PGCE curriculum contributing to students' sense of ethical agency. These aspects included immersion and guided observation in different contexts to penetrate barriers of discomfort and stereotype. Academic subjects like Sociology or Philosophy provided conceptual categories that helped to organise students' thinking about the links between school and society. Exposure to those who were succeeding against the odds challenged preconceptions and offered powerful and authentic role models that could inspire hope and motivation in the student teachers. Debates and discussions gave opportunity for the pre-service teachers to consider alternative viewpoints, and led them to a realisation of the complexity of teaching. For some, there was an acknowledgement that content and pedagogy could only provide a spark in the direction of agency, and that personal responsibility was also a key factor in the development of students' commitment and values.

Gaps in the programme with respect to preparation for a diversity of contexts included the need for greater exposure outside of a 'bubble' of privilege, stronger relationships with non-urban environments, lecturers who were more closely connected to the contemporary challenges of schooling in South Africa, and – most often mentioned – the need and desire for more confidence with practical classroom strategies.

Conclusion

This chapter aimed to explore ways to develop the deeper purposes of situated judgement and ethical agency in a single programme, the PGCE at Stellenbosch University. I explored how the purpose and design of the Practical Learning module of the PGCE linked to the ways in which the module was presented. To move beyond an intended curriculum and better understand the implemented curriculum, the second part of the chapter reported on which (if any) concepts, theories or approaches students found meaningful in their own preparation for a diversity of contexts. Such an account provides a small example of an attempt to teach for educational virtuosity, "trying to see how it functions, how it is embodied, where it is done explicitly, where it is held back" (Biesta, 2015:21).

Tentative conclusions from students' observation reports and interviews indicated that students had an acute awareness of the link between education and society. Overwhelmingly – at least for those who were interviewed – they saw the PGCE as providing an opportunity for growth and challenge within the South African context, even though certain limitations of the programme in this regard were clearly articulated. Linking back to the notion of ethical agency, one could say that students had a strong ethical orientation, but a hesitant sense of agency, the latter due to doubts about their competence in practical classroom strategies to deal with diverse learners and contexts.

Design-based research sets out to implement and research an intervention, and to draw out principles for further improvement of that intervention. In line with this, the chapter ends with suggesting a set of curriculum principles that might be considered in support of the goals of the module. Drawing on the findings of this small study, I would argue that the development of ethical agency for teaching is an intertwining of awareness, responsibility, immersion and action. This resonates strongly with the concept of 'embodiment' as an alternative to trying to bridge the so-called gap between theory and practice in learning to teach. Rather, it would seem to be the experience of the different interlinked aspects of becoming a teacher that makes the difference, where: "knowledge [for teaching] is understood as existing in a dynamic relationship between social, psychological, material and embodied realities" (Ord & Nuttall, 2016:357). In other words, and to put it simply, good or virtuous teaching must be learnt, must be experienced, and must be felt. And at the level of the classroom, one can see that every aspect of teaching and learning matters: academic content, pedagogy, experience, observation, as well as student histories and aspirations.

References

Amin, N. & Ramrathan, P. 2009. Preparing students to teach in and for diverse contexts: A learning to teach approach. *Perspectives in Education*, 27(1):69-77.

Biesta, G.J.J. 2015. How does a competent teacher become a good teacher? On judgement, wisdom and virtuosity in teaching and teacher education. In: R. Heilbronn & L. Foreman-Peck (eds), *Philosophical perspectives on teacher education*. Chichester: Wiley-Blackwell, pp. 3-22. https://doi.org/10.1002/9781118977859.ch1

Cochran-Smith, M. 2004. *Walking the road: Race, diversity, and social justice in teacher education*. New York: Teachers College Press.

DHET (Department of Higher Education and Training). 2015. *Revised policy on the minimum requirements for teacher education qualifications*. Government Gazette No 38487. Pretoria, South Africa: Department of Higher Education and Training.

Gore, J., Griffiths, T. & Ladwig, J. 2004. Towards better teaching: Productive pedagogy as a framework for teacher education. *Teaching and Teacher Education*, 20(4):375-387. https://doi.org/10.1016/j.tate.2004.02.010

Green, B., Reid, J.A. & Brennan, M. 2017. Challenging policy, rethinking practice: Struggling for the soul of teacher education. In: T.A. Trippestad, A. Swennan & T. Werler (eds), *The struggle for teacher education: International perspectives on governance and reform*. London and New York: Bloomsbury, pp. 39-55. https://doi.org/10.5040/9781474285568.0008

Herrington, J. & Reeves, T.C. 2011. Using design principles to improve pedagogical practice and promote student engagement. In: G. Williams, P. Statham, N. Brown & B. Cleland (eds), *Changing demands, changing directions*. Proceedings ascilite Hobart 2011, pp. 594-601.

Hordern, J. 2018. Is powerful educational knowledge possible? *Cambridge Journal of Education*, 48(6):787-802. https://doi.org/10.1080/0305764X.2018.1427218

Kemmis, S. 2018. Life in practices: Challenges for education and educational research. In: C. Edwards-Groves, P. Grootenboer & J. Wilkinson (eds), *Education in an era of schooling*. Singapore: Springer, pp. 239-254. https://doi.org/10.1007/978-981-13-2053-8_16

Max, C. 2010. Learning-for-teaching across educational boundaries. In: V. Ellis, A. Edwards & P. Smagorinsky (eds), *Cultural-historical perspectives on teacher education and development*. London: Routledge, pp. 212-240.

Ord, K. & Nuttall, J. 2016. Bodies of knowledge: The concept of embodiment as an alternative to theory/practice debates in the preparation of teachers. *Teaching and Teacher Education*, 60:355-362. https://doi.org/10.1016/j.tate.2016.05.019

Robinson, M. 2014. Selecting teaching practice schools across social contexts: Conceptual and policy challenges from South Africa. *Journal of Education for Teaching: International research and pedagogy*, 40(2):114-127. https://doi.org/10.1080/02607476.2013.869970

Shulman, L. 2004. *The wisdom of practice: Essays on teaching, learning and learning to teach*. San Francisco: Jossey-Bass.

Stellenbosch University. *Strategy for teaching and learning: 2017–2021.* https://bit.ly/3l1BLjk [accessed 12 May 2020].

Winch, C. 2017. *Teachers' know-how: a philosophical investigation.* Oxford: Wiley-Blackwell. https://doi.org/10.1002/9781119355700

Zembylas, M. 2003. Interrogating "teacher identity": Emotion, resistance, and self-formation. *Educational Theory*, 53(1):107-127. https://doi.org/10.1111/j.1741-5446.2003.00107.x

Zeichner, K. 2009. *Teacher education and the struggle for social justice.* New York: Routledge. https://doi.org/10.4324/9780203878767

Teaching educational psychology: Creating an epistemological disposition

Karlien Conradie

Introduction

The discipline of educational psychology is one of the core areas of interest in the Postgraduate Certificate in Education (PGCE) offered by the Faculty of Education at Stellenbosch University, and is deemed essential for understanding the processes of learning, supporting and teaching, especially in the context of adolescence.

The revised *Policy on the Minimum Requirements for Teacher Education Qualifications* (DHET, 2015) refers to five types of learning associated with the acquisition, integration and application of knowledge for teaching purposes. These types of learning underpin the design of programmes leading to teacher education qualifications (see section 3.4 of the revised policy, 2015). One of these types of learning, namely disciplinary learning, is vital for positioning educational psychology as a significant foundation of education. The policy defines disciplinary learning as: "disciplinary knowledge which can be presented in the study of education and its foundations, including but not limited to the philosophy, psychology, politics, economics, sociology and history of education" (DHET, 2015:11). Educational psychology is an indispensable disciplinary means of accessing knowledge and understanding of the relational or connected nature of being and acting in the world. It provides the kind of disciplinary insight that penetrates to the socio-emotional core of human development, which in turn forms the foundation of a child's capacity to learn and a teacher's conscious capacity to be sensitively responsive to processes of learning, reflecting and understanding.

Although the minimum qualification required for entry to the PGCE programme is a bachelor's degree, admission seldom requires a deep understanding of the disciplinary knowledge associated with developmental psychology. It may be assumed that many candidate teacher students are not academically experienced in deep content pertaining to human development, such as attachment or affectional bonding, interpersonal trust, motivation and self-regulation, to name but a few of the psychological matters that underlie the process of learning.

In this chapter, I attempt to organise some of the main theoretical dimensions and principles that constitute my own epistemological foundation. This foundation evolved from my formal studies and experience in the disciplines and practice of teaching and psychology. To encourage students to delve into the delicate and respectful craft of mediated learning, I have to map some of the central and linking aspects underlying the learning relationship. I explain these aspects, including emotional security (trust), healthy psychological boundaries, interconnectedness and individuation, as well as the role teachers can play as ad hoc attachment figures[1] in simulating attachment security. Prominent researchers in the field of attachment theory have pointed out that the function of a secure affectional bond is to ensure a flourishing and individuated[2] sense of self. This in turn leads to the trusting relationship between adult and child, including that between teacher and learner, which is

---

1   Researchers in the field of attachment, including Kennedy and Kennedy (2004), regard teachers as ad hoc attachment figures because the teacher-child attachment, unlike the child-primary caregiver attachment, is relatively short-lived and a less exclusive emotional investment.

2   Individuation refers to the gradual process of integrating opposite archetypal functions and elements, such as chaos and order, creation and destruction, death and rebirth, growth and regression, good and evil, anima and animus, individuality and collectivity. In the Jungian tradition, the process of individuation serves to maintain a healthy tension between ambivalent content from which vitality and creativity (growth) can spring. In the words of Carl Jung: "The ego keeps its integrity only if it does not identify with one of the opposites, and if it understands how to hold the balance between them. This is possible only if it remains conscious of both at once" (1960:para 425).

critically important for human growth and learning. It appears that a tapestry of disciplinary insight into human development and the process of learning is indispensable for ethical education praxis. Such an interpretation framework should therefore be included in the PGCE teacher education and training curriculum as part of a core module that emphasises educational psychology.

Contributing to the science of teacher education

Educational psychology is considered a branch of the broader field of psychology and is mainly concerned with the process of human learning in various educational settings (Swart & Eloff, 2019:2-3). It typically spans dimensions of the scientific study of learning challenges and educational interventions, as well as the associated role of psychosocial factors. The contribution of educational psychology to education is also found in its strong links with other social sciences relevant to education, such as philosophy, psychology and, of course, education itself (Norwich, 2002).

The discipline of educational psychology draws from other core disciplines, such as psychology, education and philosophy, to deal with a number of critical developmental and educational matters. With regard to teaching and training, these matters include high-school educators' insight into the different developmental dimensions of adolescent learning (such as neurology, cognition, motivation, personality and socio-emotional development), and the promotion of supportive and nourishing learning environments. The focus would therefore be on certain human characteristics, for example intelligence, cognitive development, affect (emotions, feelings, and mood), motivation and self-regulation, as well as academic self-concept and its role in learning.

Educational psychology is concerned with the way development, learning, teaching and environment intersect with one another to promote or inhibit educational growth and thriving. The goals, therefore, are to gain critical insight into the teaching and learning processes in everyday situations, such as general living, schooling, studying and working, and to improve them (Norwich, 2002). The prominent place the module occupies in the PGCE programme puts it in an excellent position to expose students to some of the key dimensions underlying the processes of learning and teaching in secondary education, such as adolescent development, motivation, mediation, self-efficacy, self-regulation, cognitive strategies, intervention and support, as well as social, emotional and behavioural challenges in the classroom. These dimensions are knitted together to form the module content and serve as an essential psychoeducational foundation for the aspiring secondary-phase education student. However, to preserve the epistemological significance of curriculum knowledge, the teaching approach followed in such a module is important. Any teaching approach, including thinking and making choices about the composition and facilitation of the curriculum, implies a preceding epistemological disposition. An epistemological disposition refers to the possible character of knowledge and consists of certain core theoretical insights and philosophical views that serve as the framework for understanding and arguing specific curriculum knowledge. I have over the last few years endeavoured to develop an initial, integrated epistemological disposition which serves to be the foundation of my approach to teaching educational psychology to PGCE students.

Teaching educational psychology: Framing language, disciplinary insights and theoretical views

The rationale or basis of an intellectual position or practice often is a particular thought framework. Such a framework usually comprises certain paradigmatic viewpoints, philosophical orientations and theoretical principles that open up ways of understanding discourses, problems and phenomena. Moss (2019:28) explains: "Paradigms affect our thinking about everything, including ontology (What is reality?), epistemology (How do you know something?) and methodology (How do you go about finding out?)". My view of humanity and the phenomena of development and learning precede what and how I teach. This view is informed by related disciplinary knowledge and theoretical orientations in the broader field of psychology and education. The particular assemblage of ideas provides the guiding principle on the basis of which an intellectually grounding tapestry of curriculum knowledge can be carefully woven. It also anchors a module that focuses on educational psychology as part of the offering of a professional teacher education programme such as PGCE. Although this process is continuously evolving, I have tried to weave a tapestry that may become a grounding for this particular module and includes the theoretical aspects of attachment, care, interconnectedness and individuation.

The following section presents my preliminary synthesis of some of the core disciplinary insights and theoretical principles that underlie the module I teach (see Figure 3.1). Through logical argumentation, the insights and principles are merged into a particular pattern of thought that functions potentially as an epistemological disposition for teaching educational psychology.

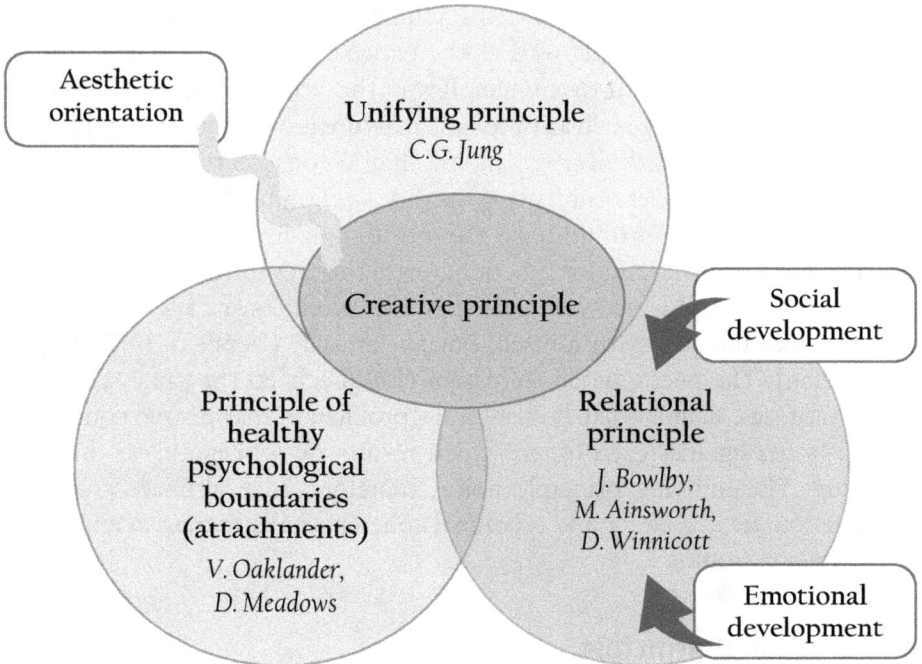

Figure 3.1 Preliminary synthesis of some of the core disciplinary insights and theoretical principles underlying the educational psychology module in the PGCE at Stellenbosch University

The unifying principle

The Jungian understanding of human development, based on the revolutionary work of Carl Gustav Jung (1875–1961), reflects a gnostic orientation that views everything and everyone as inherently interconnected and part of a larger whole. The relevance of such a unifying principle does not depend on whether or not it is credible in a religion – in other words, a belief in a larger cosmic coherence. It rather proposes decentring the human being as an exceptional and independent ruling entity. A unified view, characterised by implied interdependence and relational embeddedness, disputes such an anthropocentric notion of being human. For Jung (1958/2002) this means, for example, that when human beings harm any aspect of the natural world, they harm a part of their larger selves (33-34). The notion of human exceptionality corresponds to the Cartesian ideal of human immortality that can only be attained through a self-indulgent consumerist approach driven by ceaseless *amor concupiscentiae* (devouring desires, power, status, money, etc.). Marthinus Versfeld (1982), a South African philosopher who wrote movingly about the ontological nature of being human, was convinced that such an instrumentalist ethos is followed at the expense of the innate need for an intimate connection with that which lies in the realm of human experience and beyond. To develop such an ontological nature is of particular significance in this era of unbridled, ever-expanding digital consumerism characterised by fragmentation, over-stimulation, utility and immediacy. Without an embedded view of humankind and the world, individuals and communities will become mere ungrounded functionaries of the prevailing societal zeitgeist that emphasises thoughtless pursuit of power, products and pleasure. Such a person "does not live with himself, but *for* himself" (Versfeld, 1982:61) [my translation]. The poet Charles Bernstein (1986) echoed the same sentiment in his writings, namely that humankind's problem is that people constantly set up issues against each other, which results in 'schismatic' or dualistic thinking. The unifying principle holds, therefore, that ultimate creativity and freedom lie in a larger and relational coherence, rather than in entities of conformist reasoning.

The relational principle

The caring, receptive disposition begins with the premise that as humans we are inherently relational, responsive beings. The human condition is therefore one of connectedness and interdependence in which we experience ourselves in relation to others but do not dismiss individual psychological and social boundaries. The evolutionary function of human beings to elicit care from primary others is called attachment. This function starts to develop even before birth and before any other learning can take place. Secure attachments, that is, affectional bonds, are formed when caregivers are deeply and sensitively attuned to a child's need for physical safety, psychological security, proximity, comfort, care, warmth and loving interaction. Such attachments result in a sense of being grounded, characterised by familiarity and predictability, which in turn encourage responsible risk-taking, exploration and creativity. The pioneering attachment researchers John Bowlby and Mary Ainsworth (cited in Van der Horst, 2011) theorised that early experiences with primary caregivers are particularly important for the development of secure attachment relationships and the formation of a person's own future attachment (including parenting or teaching) style. Noteworthy is the sentiment of embodiment, which means the internal working model or schema of a relationship is initially grounded in a physical or sensory experience of being in the world.

Infants' expressed desire for proximity is dependent on caregivers' past responses to them (Geddes, 2006). If caregivers' responding styles are mainly characterised by rigid, cold and distant or laissez-faire behaviour, children will eventually learn that adults will not take care of or comfort them. Infants are born with a propensity to direct attachment behaviours such as crying, clinging and looking at the caregivers who are most likely to respond. These behaviours elicit caregiving and bring the caregiver into close proximity with the infant, ensuring protection from environmental dangers and a sense of security (evolutionary function). Over time, infants begin to direct these responses primarily to one or a few caregivers, and at around seven to eight months of age, infants show attachment to caregivers by protesting their leaving and grieving for them during their absence (Bergin & Bergin, 2009; Geddes, 2006). During this time, young children form an internal working model of the attachment relationships which serves as an internal representation of the self, others and relationships (e.g. self as competent and worthy of respect; others as guiding, supportive, helpful) (Kennedy & Kennedy, 2004).

A secure base depends on the child's internal working model of caregivers as trustworthy, sensitive, accessible and responsive to their needs. Since children's behaviour and intentions often reflect their relationship history and strategies for coping with stress and relatedness, it is essential that attachment security be established through deliberate education and nurturance (Bergin & Bergin, 2009; Geddes, 2006). Close emotional relationships can also exist beyond the child-parent or child-primary caregiver attachment, e.g. the teacher-child relationship, in which teachers are regarded as ad hoc attachment figures. In such a case, the teacher-child relationship may allow for exploration from a secure base and for a safe haven in stressful situations. In this way the relationship will have a positive influence on socio-emotional development (Kennedy & Kennedy, 2004).

Social development precedes emotional development

Socio-emotional development is typically seen as a complicated and gradual process, driven by the a priori phenomenon of attachment – the innate need to establish intimate connections with others and the world in which one exists. This includes matters such as emotional regulation (having insight into one's own and others' emotional reactions), empathy and the development of personal identity. Furthermore, there is a significant link between cognitive and social development in the sense that a person's cognitive skills and capacities cannot be fully engaged unless the need for intimate bonding and emotional security (trust) is nurtured. Secure attachment relationships correlate strongly with higher academic attainment, socio-emotional insight and competence, including empathy and self-regulation (Bergin & Bergin, 2009; Geddes, 2006). It is not for nothing that the distinguished psychologist Donald Winnicott repeatedly made a powerful case for the delicate, fundamental mechanism of the child-caretaker bond, which forms the basis for interdependent behaviour that is characterised by an awareness and recognition of the simultaneous nature of one's individual autonomy (freedom) and one's embeddedness in the collective world of everything.

Emotional development is not a natural developmental occurrence; it occurs only with deliberate and optimal nurturance and education. If the emotional development of children is neglected, they often become adults that struggle to build loving long-term relationships (Bergin & Bergin, 2009). The way in which parents as primary caregivers, and other attachment figures such as teachers, initially and over time respond to children's needs largely guides their emotional development. Researchers in the field of child development agree that the emotional caring style (e.g. rigid, cold, warm, laissez-faire, authoritative, democratic, stable) of the adult precedes the child's own developing emotional repertoire. If the adult's emotional caring style is characterised by unconditional acceptance, consistency and predictability, recognition and love, it forms the foundation of a trusting attachment between the child and the caregiver. It should be noted that love in this sense is not of a sentimental nature, but rather an uninhibited and generous way of being open and attuned – being unquestionably present – to the needs of the developing child. When the emotional caring style of an adult is instead characterised by inconsistency and conditionality, it creates enormous confusion and uncertainty in any child. In essence, this kind of behaviour by adults towards children signifies the violation of an important psychosocial boundary, namely that between the adult as the carer and the child as the care-recipient. While it is expected of the adult to be the caregiver, the child, because of his or her natural (developmental) vulnerability, is allowed to expect proper care from an adult.

When children's innate developmental vulnerability and trusting nature are manipulated and exploited by an uncaring and unresponsive society, they are robbed of a sense of security. What such children learn is that relationships are mainly good in so far as one gets something out of them for one's own advancement and survival. In turn, such a distorted orientation towards relationships has the potential to lead to manipulation and exploitation by the child. Consequently, such a child's own emotional repertoire will over time be characterised predominantly by fear, suspicion, distrust and repressed anger.

This limited emotional repertoire, which rests on an inadequate attachment with primary caregivers, will continue to play itself out by being projected on to other relationships in the form of resistant, avoidant or disorganised (chaotic) behaviour. It is this kind of expressed behaviour by both adult (including the teacher student) and child that often is observed in school classrooms and lecture halls. One can come to understand and intervene in this attachment phenomenon by means of a combination of attachment theory and general systems thinking, as well as the principles of gestalt and Jungian analytical psychology.

In the following sections, I describe how this cluster of theoretical orientations may be applied to establish further the relational argument and the rest of the proposed epistemological disposition.

The principle of healthy psychological boundaries

In the context of systems thinking and according to the principles of pioneering gestalt and Jungian analytical psychology, it is in the interest of the natural integrity of human beings to constantly cultivate preservative and functional boundaries. This would mean that the individual and the collective – as interconnected and complex self-organising systems or environments, each made up of different processes, characteristics, events and circumstances – continuously strive to maintain equilibrium. Donnella Meadows (2008) is renowned for her work in the field of systems thinking, and uses this approach to understand phenomena pertaining to the human condition. She considers that the capacity for self-correction and self-support of any system implies the focus should be on the enhancement of wholeness and integration. Jung's view of the self, as a fundamental psychic ordering principle essential for self-regulation, is similar (1916/1960). Even before any learning takes place, the human endeavour is to become psychologically grounded. To achieve this, it is essential to satisfy especially the primordial psychic need for personal relationships, group belonging, recognition, new experiences, self-efficacy and spiritual connections, as extensively described by the psychoanalysts John Bowlby, Mary Ainsworth and Donald Winnicott (cited in Van der Horst, 2011).

Arising from the above is the capacity, attributed to proximal and more indirect relationships and interactions of both an intra- and interpersonal nature, to gain awareness of how influences are related to the current state of affairs, difficulties or the contemporary zeitgeist. This focus on one's autonomy and understanding oneself as simultaneously apart from and part of the external world, is one of the basic assumptions in gestalt psychology. Underlying this assumption is perhaps the human instinct to learn (survive), which in turn is driven by one's need to have one's own identity and be accepted by others. This gives rise to the question: Where do I start and where do I end? In the context of healthy emotional and social development, the sense of the differentiated self (a sense of self) is achieved through understanding and applying clearly defined psychological boundaries. Because of their developmental level, characterised by natural receptiveness and openness to explore, children and adolescents are more vulnerable to the manipulation and violation of their own boundaries.

Generally, various types of boundaries can be identified, such as individual, intergenerational and family boundaries, each characterised by certain states, ranging from too strong (rigid), to healthy (flexible) to too weak (diffuse) (Friel & Friel, 1988). Human beings' primordial need for acceptance by others has already been mentioned. It is perhaps not surprising that "the underlying reason that individuals can't set healthy limits is that they are desperately afraid that they will be abandoned if they say *no*" (Friel & Friel, 1988:59). The principle of confluence, a key term in gestalt psychology, refers to a boundless state. Violet Oaklander (cited in Campbell, 1993:59), an expert child therapist, explains this as:

> [...] not having a good sense of self, when someone doesn't have a sense of who they are without knowing what the other thinks of them or children who seem to be very enmeshed with their parents, or are overly eager to please.

When the lines between adults and children, and between individuals and groups, become vague or even violated through projection, guilt, isolation and manipulation, the individual is robbed of a sense of safety and learns that they will not be cared for. As a result, children and young people start either to block their own emotions or to display emotionally irrational behaviour. This in turn inhibits contact, another key gestalt term, which Oaklander (cited in Campbell, 1993:58) explains as the ability to be aware of "what one feels, being congruent with what one is feeling, and using the intellect, speaking and expressing through the intellect as part of making contact". The principle of healthy psychological boundaries is summarised in Figure 3.2.

Cultivating a healthy psychological fence

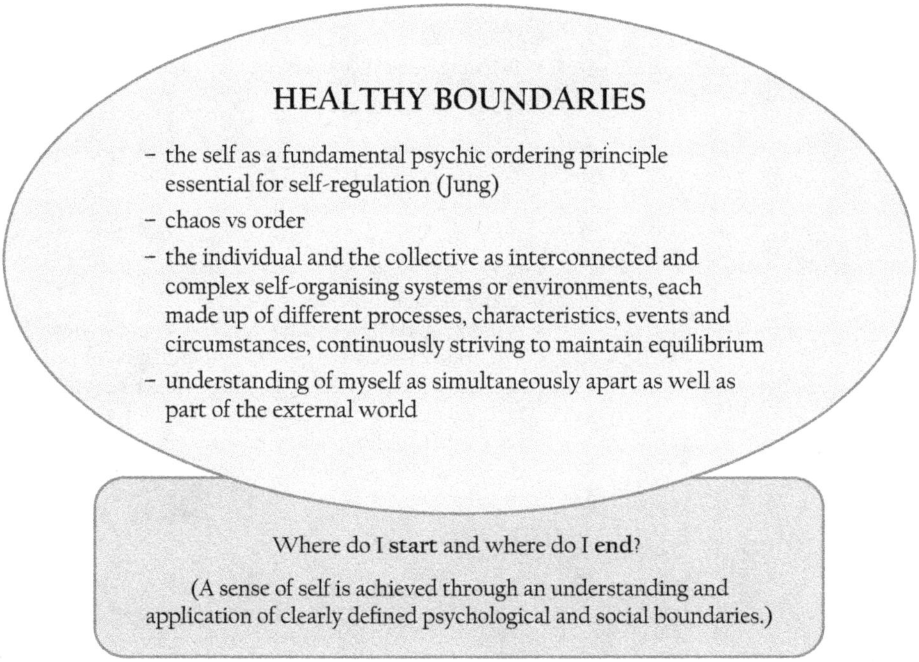

HEALTHY BOUNDARIES

- the self as a fundamental psychic ordering principle essential for self-regulation (Jung)
- chaos vs order
- the individual and the collective as interconnected and complex self-organising systems or environments, each made up of different processes, characteristics, events and circumstances, continuously striving to maintain equilibrium
- understanding of myself as simultaneously apart as well as part of the external world

Where do I **start** and where do I **end**?

(A sense of self is achieved through an understanding and application of clearly defined psychological and social boundaries.)

Figure 3.2   The principle of healthy psychological boundaries

Promoting and stimulating nurturing rituals and rhythms characterised by a contemplative orientation, silence and consistency allows for circumstantial movement (without using defence mechanisms) between psychological and social boundaries. In modern society, communication is characterised by broadcasting, utility and immediacy, a mass human machine where nothing ever really stops or starts, begins or ends. Healthy boundaries are threatened even more. In such circumstances, the inherent developmental vulnerability of children and adolescents may lead to them finding it difficult not to overflow (loss of individual autonomy or personal integrity) or wither within their own boundaries (Kirschner & De Bruyckere, 2017). To counter this challenge, classrooms and teaching practices can imitate healthy boundaries and attachments to stimulate and promote optimal emotional, and therefore social, development. However, it requires that teachers (and student teachers) consider the psychic life of the developing child, as well as their own relational histories in an intellectual and analytical manner. The specific boundary states described are presented in Figure 3.3.

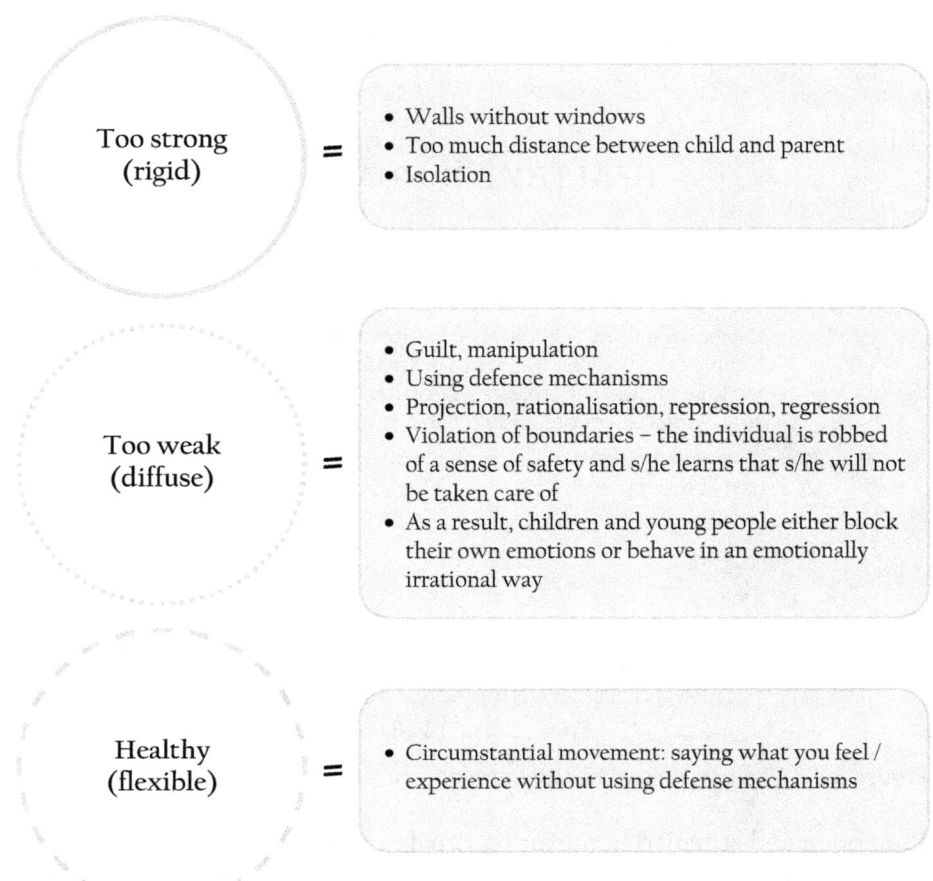

Figure 3.3 Boundary states (adapted from Friel & Friel, 1988)

Teachers, schools and communities have to provide a sense of psychological safety, that is, emotional security, as opposed to engendering insecure, anxious feelings. A secure base is needed for healthy risk-taking and exploration. Setting appropriate and clear boundaries in a consistent and predictable manner is a way of being empathic and aids the establishment of emotional security. Regular rituals and repetitive routines (healthy rhythms) are grounding by nature and can lay the foundation for proper self-regulation, intellectual development, inner calmness and control, identity and values. These are routines that are not too rigid or strict, rather adaptable and spontaneous, and can include regular reading and writing hours, conversation circles, visits to museums, the theatre and art galleries, strolls in botanical gardens and hiking. At the core of these physical and sensory actions lies the potential of a more conscious connection with oneself, allowing one to gain better insight into one's own embedded nature and place in the larger cosmos.

The creative principle

In my view, the creative principle serves as the intersection of all the other theoretical viewpoints and is inferred from the Jungian principle of individuation. Individuation, in Jungian terms, refers to the innate human potential for creating a state of psychological equilibrium by integrating manifold inner contradictions into a unified totality. It means to seek out actively (to recognise), and become aware of, opposite elements (e.g. feelings, thoughts, orientations, urges and needs), and to discover how they all form part of a unitary and integrated cosmos beyond mere binaries, hierarchies and independent entities. Individuation is a lifelong process during which the human psyche attempts naturally to maintain and preserve the delicate balance between simultaneous and conflicting possibilities of an ontological nature, such as life and death, destruction and creation, masculinity and femininity, inclusion and exclusion, individual and culture, and order and chaos. The Jungian view is that vitality, imagination and creativity spring from the incongruity of opposite elements, developing wholeness. At the core of my theoretical disposition is the strong conviction that the human psyche is naturally directed at continuously developing greater psychological consciousness, that is, the constant integration of psychic opposites into a meaningful entirety.

According to the Jungian point of view, a free society depends on the increased consciousness of the individuals that make up that society. As Jung puts it: "[I]f the individual is not truly regenerated in spirit, society cannot be either, for society is the sum total of individuals in need of redemption" (1958/2002:40). An ethical endeavour would therefore be to nurture the a priori potential for development and growth that resides in individuals and eventually in communities, and at the same time to refute the dogmatic mass-mindedness that sees the individual as a mere function of society.

The aesthetic orientation as an underlying transcendental function of education

Closely associated with the creative principle is the aesthetic orientation, which suggests a certain quality of experience – a heightened sensory awareness and hence a change of consciousness. Aesthetics refers to the Greek understanding of *aesthēsis*, which alludes to a sharpened ability to distinguish between subtle changes and to observe interrelated possibilities, unexpected influences and the simultaneousness of everything. It can be argued that, besides the cognitive dimension, the quality of that which is comprehended depends on the sensory and affective dimensions of understanding. Research has confirmed that the quality of our thinking, problem-solving skills, creativity, imagination, initiative and emotional and social insight originates from the physical or bodily experience (Johnson, 1987; Krantz, 1994). Emerson, who wrote magnificently about aesthetics, states that beauty can be seen as: "the virtue which constitutes a thing beautiful," that is, "a certain cosmical quality, or, a power to suggest relation to the whole world, and so lifts the object out of a pitiful individuality" (1983:1110-1111). In contrast to individualism is the Jungian concept of individuation, that is, self-transformation or the process of becoming who you are. Individuation refers to a visceral awareness of human fellowship and the interdependence of all events, objects and creatures. The aesthetic orientation provides an antidote to what Stiegler (cited in Ieven, 2012) refers to as the hyper-industrialised society. This term denotes the increasing marketability and commodification of everything. In light of this view, it can be argued that the aesthetic orientation, characterised by contemplative silence, sharpened attentiveness, patience and imagination, contributes to a deeper and renewed (transformed) experience of understanding (knowing) and being in the world.

Module outcome and content

On completion of this module, the intention is that pre-service teachers should have gained critical insight into the developmental phase of adolescence and how developmental dimensions interact with the learning process and influence teaching practice, including effective mediation and support of diverse learning abilities. Based on the rationale and outcome of this module the curriculum consists of the following themes and foci:

1. Educational psychology explained as the intersection of Psychology, Philosophy and Education;
2. The adolescent developmental phase and implications for the classroom. (Bronfenbrenner's bio-ecological model as a way of understanding human development in terms of a multitude of reciprocal influences, variables and processes; physical and neurological development in the adolescent developmental phase; cognitive development and psychosocial development);
3. The experience of learning as an embedded process (Various learning theories, discourses and teaching dispositions, including artful teaching; learning preferences and strategies; and complex cognitive strategies, including critical thinking, problem-solving, meta-learning and self-regulated learning);
4. The teacher as mediator of embedded learning experiences (Mediation of learning; teaching modalities and strategies; creating aesthetic learning experiences and environments; motivation);

5. Inclusive education and learning support (Defining inclusive education; assessing for learning support; specific learning barriers; educational intervention); and
6. Social, emotional and behavioural challenges in the classroom (Definition, nature and types of social, emotional and behavioural challenges; supporting such challenges through preventative care and empathic intervention).

The educational meaningfulness of the discipline-specific content listed above is based on the epistemological theorems which I have explained earlier. As student teachers gradually immerse themselves in the module content over the course of the year, I urge them to try to identify some important psychoeducational principles from each of the above-mentioned themes. This requires students to formulate and substantiate various succinct fundamental rules, laws or propositions derived from the themes concerned. Finally, they need to describe in practical terms how the different principles can be applied in the learning and teaching environment. Such an assignment does not only assess students' knowledge and understanding of the content, but also stimulates the emergence of an integrated network of connected discipline-specific insights that can act as a theoretical framework.

Challenges and affordances closely associated with teaching educational psychology in the PGCE programme

Teaching educational psychology to pre-service high school teachers affords the opportunity to place learning and support against the backdrop of human development, specifically adolescence, and to highlight very specific implications for learning and teaching in contemporary educational settings. Teaching educational psychology affords an inside track into understanding students' own psychological challenges and needs, and the opportunity to provide support where possible. In fact, the curriculum often unintentionally addresses some of the challenges and needs that occur by applying cognitive strategies more effectively, and identifying and evaluating unhelpful, that is, rigid or intellectually immature, mental schemas, amongst other things.

One of the challenges in teaching educational psychology is that the discipline itself regularly holds up a mirror to students. This often causes socially and emotionally immature students, or students with unresolved disappointments and psychological issues, to project possible inadequate past experiences onto their current learning and teaching situation. Such reactions often reflect students' longstanding and unresolved past experiences, taking the form of inflexible thinking, excessive emotional outbursts, intolerance of disciplinary knowledge and extrinsic blaming and shaming. Over time, such circumstances may unfortunately give rise to an attitude characterised mainly by distrust and suspicion, to which the student reverts by default in stressful times. Such a debilitating orientation holds serious negative consequences for the student's ability to be receptive to new learning experiences and opportunities. It should perhaps also be kept in mind that the initial learning approach of students in the developmental stage of early adulthood is normally characterised by reactivity and the mere repetition of existing ways of thinking (Taylor, 2000:157-158). The continuous process of learning and meaning-making implies regular adjustment, change and re-creation (transformation) of what is currently believed or known. This is perhaps best done by way of critical and thoughtful reflection.

The sociologist and educator Jack Mezirow (2000), in his theoretical views on transformative learning, emphasises the process of reflective thinking and reconsideration of existing thinking schemes and discourses through critical evaluation and reformulation. For Mezirow, it is mainly about development of a critical awareness of the way in which environmental influences work together to transform one's own assumptions and beliefs over time into a specific meaning scheme or world view. That world view usually influences one's behaviour and actions, and the way one evaluates and makes sense of the self, others and the world of which one forms part. Transformative learning assumes that limiting thinking frameworks can be adapted, modified and expanded through deliberate reflection and elaboration to include alternative insights. This process of perspective transformation further presupposes that the intellectual (thinking) function is thoroughly interwoven with the function of the affective (emotion, feeling, motivation and intentionality), and indicates the totality of the meaning of an experience.

Transformative learning implies reformulation and involves a reflective process, in other words, critical reflection on an experience as a whole. It therefore includes thoughts, ideas, sensations, feelings, reactions, decisions and actions. Characteristic prerequisites of the reflective process include the ability to be open to all aspects of an experience, the application of *epoché* (a Greek philosophical term referring to the temporary suspension of a validation or judgement), association formation and the eventual synthesis of different views. One can agree with David Boud (cited in Boud, Keogh & Walker, 1985), therefore, when he remarks: "Reflection is an important human activity in which people recapture their experience, think about it, mull it over and evaluate. It is this working with experience that is important in learning" (1985:19). Transformative learning, however, is a sophisticated and continuous deployment process that includes intellectual (abstract and multiple thinking) and affective (ability for openness, empathy and maintaining relationships with others) maturity.

Conclusion

In this chapter, I have attempted to reflect on the questions: How do I approach the teaching of my PGCE module in educational psychology? And, why do I choose this way? This reflection included describing what educational psychology entails in the context of teaching, as well as an exposition of how the module content is organised according to themes and associated foci. Reflecting on the question about a specific approach is prompted by the need to explain and map the significance of educational psychology in understanding the delicate mediating relationship between teacher and learner. Becoming a teacher who seeks to enter the learning relationship in an attentive and sensitively responsive manner demands an understanding of the development of secure attachment relationships. In countries such as South Africa, where relationships are often characterised by fear, suspicion, distrust and repressed anger, this may be even more necessary. I should like to believe that educational psychology is in an excellent position to heed this call because of its ability to illuminate essential dimensions of human development and the process of learning. Thinking in this way has led me to synthesise some key theoretical principles and disciplinary insights, which resulted in an initial epistemological disposition. This continuously evolving locus forms the foundation of my teaching of educational psychology to students who want to be teachers. The importance of an initial epistemological disposition is perhaps twofold. Synthesising related theoretical principles and disciplinary insights is a way of promoting a more nuanced and thoughtful educational psychology curriculum that would include conscious awareness of the challenges and affordances closely associated with teaching this particular module. It can also serve as a basis for continued improvement and refinement of the curriculum as part of the greater pedagogical quest characterised by scientific and scholarly endeavours aimed at transcendental goodness, beauty and truth.

References

Bergin, C. & Bergin, D. 2009. Attachment in the classroom. *Educational Psychology Review*, 21:141-170. https://doi.org/10.1007/s10648-009-9104-0

Bernstein, C. 1986. *Content's dream*. Los Angeles: Sun and Moon.

Boud, D., Keogh, R. & Walker, D. 1985. *Reflection: Turning experience into learning*. New York: Kogan Page.

Campbell, C.A. 1993. Interview with Violet Oaklander, author of 'Windows to our children'. *Elementary School Guidance & Counselling*, 28(1):52-61. https://doi.org/146.232.129.75

DHET (Department of Higher Education and Training). 2015. *Policy on the minimum requirements for teacher education qualifications (Revised)*. Government Gazette (No 38487), 596, February. Pretoria: Government Printer.

Emerson, R.W. 1983. *Essays and lectures*. New York: The Library of America.

Friel, J.C. & Friel, L.D. 1988. *Adult children: The secrets of dysfunctional families*. Florida: Health Communications.

Geddes, H. 2006. *Attachment in the classroom: The links between children's early experience, emotional wellbeing and performance in school*. London: Worth Publishing.

Ieven, B. 2012. The forgetting of aesthetics: Individuation, technology, and aesthetics in the work of Bernard Stiegler. *New Formations*, 77(5):7696. https://doi.org/10.3898/NEWF.77.05.2012

Johnson, M. 1987. *The body in the mind: The bodily basis of meaning, imagination and reason*. Chicago: University of Chicago Press. https://doi.org/10.7208/chicago/9780226177847.001.0001

Jung, C.G. 1916/1960. *The transcendent function. The structure and dynamics of the psyche* [The collected works of C.G. Jung]. (R.F.C. Hull, transl.). New York: Pantheon Books.

Jung, C.G. (1958/2002). *The undiscovered self*. London: Routledge & Paul.

Kennedy, J.H. & Kennedy, C.E. 2004. Attachment theory: Implications for school psychology. *Psychology in Schools*, 41(12):247-259. https://doi.org/10.1002/pits.10153

Kirschner, P.A. & De Bruyckere, P. 2017. The myths of the digital native and the multitasker. *Teaching and Teacher Education*, 67:135-142. https://doi.org/10.1016/j.tate.2017.06.001

Krantz, M. 1994. *Child development*. Belmont, California: Wadsworth.

Meadows, D. 2008. *Thinking in systems*. Vermont: Chelsea Green Publishing.

Mezirow, J. 2000. *Learning as transformation: Critical perspectives on a theory in progress*. San Francisco: Jossey-Bass.

Moss, P. 2019. *Alternative narratives in early childhood: An introduction for students and practitioners*. New York: Routledge. https://doi.org/10.4324/9781315265247

Norwich, B. 2002. *Education and psychology in interaction*. London: Routledge. https://doi.org/10.4324/9780203464793

Swart, E. & Eloff, I. 2019. Educational psychology as science and profession in South Africa. In: I. Eloff & E. Swart (eds), *Understanding educational psychology*. Cape Town: Juta, pp. 2-9.

Taylor, K. 2000. Teaching with developmental intention. In: J. Mezirow (ed.), *Learning as transformation: Critical perspectives on a theory in progress*. San Francisco: Jossey-Bass, pp. 151-180.

Van der Horst, F.C.P. 2011. *John Bowlby: From psychoanalysis to ethology*. New Jersey: Wiley-Blackwell. https://doi.org/10.1002/9781119993100

Versfeld, M. 1982. *Tyd en dae*. Cape Town: Tafelberg.

Teaching a new generation: Implications for Curriculum Studies

Marie Louise Botha

Introduction

Embarking on a journey into a new decade, the third within the first century of the third millennium, it becomes imperative to revisit initial teacher education curriculum. Specifically, we should focus on what is needed for a new generation of young people aspiring to become teachers in the twenty-first century, possibly extending into their professional development as in-service teachers. Over the last three decades changes in teaching and learning education demographics, specifically in South Africa, have become evident and relooking *who* we teach, *what* and *how* we teach has become vitally important. Factors indicating demographic changes include socio-economic characteristics of a community or population such as age, sex, race, education level, income level, marital status, occupation, religion, birth rate, death rate, average size of a family, and average age at marriage (Hodgkinson, 2001). During the last decade it also became clear that other factors that could be included here are language, disabilities, previous work experiences, political and religious affiliations. Experiences of both lecturers and students in higher education would typically include trends in technology such as the shifts to more online and mobile learning opportunities, increasing student age, students coming from industry and those who are working 35 or more hours a week to pay for education, those who have dependents and/or are single parents (The Tambellini Group, 2018). This chapter will focus on who the new generation is and how I, as the educator, need to change my thinking about teaching and learning in this modern era. Implications are presented for the subject module on Curriculum Studies in the Postgraduate Certificate in Education (PGCE) programme.

Background

Drawing on a range of literature, I reflect on my own teaching practice in the module Curriculum Studies located in the revised PGCE programme implemented in 2018. Further discussion in this chapter will be based on the reflective model of Rolfe, Freshwater and Jasper (2001), using reflective writing to address issues related to curriculum change and what knowledge and pedagogy is of most worth. Rolfe et al.'s (2001) reflective model endeavours to answer three questions: What (is the problem)? So what? and Now what?

Traditional ways of teaching have mostly dominated teaching and learning in this module over the past couple of years. This includes a lecture-centred approach where students are passively involved in learning the module content. It became evident that students were not critically engaged with the topics addressed. The question of why students were struggling to critically engage with content became profound. To answer this question I had to take a new look at the current curriculum of this module to determine its alignment with the demands of the new generation student cohort, what their needs might be and how better to assist their learning experience. I needed to consider who the students are, their backgrounds and characteristics that are obviously different to the student cohort of some years ago. I therefore embarked on this journey of self-reflection to better promote good teaching and effective learning to produce engaged and informed citizen-teachers for a future that is difficult to predict in the current crises of the global pandemic, economic inequality, and major environmental challenges.

The canonical curriculum question: What knowledge is of most worth? posed by Herbert Spencer in the nineteenth century (Broudy, 1982), became the main focus of this reflective reading and writing. What knowledge, and pedagogy (strategies/methods/approaches) is of most worth for the students enrolled in the PGCE programme, specifically in the Curriculum Studies module, to promote good teaching and learning in higher (tertiary) education, as well as school (primary and secondary) education?

A constructivist approach, according to the early twentieth century philosophers Dewey (1859–1952), Piaget (1896–1980) and Vygotsky (1896-1934) should inform our teaching practices, and this is what was aimed for in this module during the last couple of years. The recent implementation of the new PGCE programme gave an opportunity to revisit these philosophies for contemporary education. I use these social-constructivist philosophies as lenses through which I briefly reflect on my own teaching practice.

Dewey argues that education and learning are social and interactive processes; thus the educational institution itself is a social environment through which social reform can and should take place where students can thrive and where they are allowed to experience and interact with the curriculum. All students therefore should have the opportunity to take part in their own learning. Dewey does not support teaching methods that are static, advocating experiential learning instead (Dewey, 1938). Experiential learning is the process of learning through experience and is more specifically defined as "learning through reflection on doing" (Felicia, 2011:1003). The student has prior knowledge and experiences usually determined by their social and cultural contexts. Students learn by "constructing knowledge out of their own experiences" (Seifert & Sutton, 2009:47).

Piaget focuses on human development and how people make sense of the interactions between their own experiences and ideas, and how they are influenced by others (Piaget, 1971). According to Carey, Zaitchik and Bascandziev (2015), Piaget's work is based on two complementary pillars: constructivism and stage theory. Piaget's theory of constructivism allows teachers to view students as individual learners who add new concepts to their prior knowledge in order to construct, or build an understanding of subject content for themselves through interactions with others (Henson, 2003) not only in the classroom but also in society. Piaget's constructivism therefore concerns the emergence of new conceptual content for the individual (Carey et al., 2015), the educator and the student. His stage theory relates to stages of development that we move through as individuals as we gradually acquire the ability of becoming knowledgable (Huitt & Hummel, 2003). Piaget identified four stages of cognitive development that include the sensorimotor or infancy stage; the pre-operational stage referring to toddlers and early childhood; the concrete operational stage that includes elementary and early adolescence, and finally the formal operational stage that refers to adolescence and adults (Huitt & Hummel, 2003). The latter two stages are of greatest relevance to higher education as they include early adolescent-adults.

Vygotsky's (1896–1934) theory of social constructivism emphasises the importance of sociocultural learning; how interactions with adults, more capable peers, and cognitive tools are internalised by learners to form mental constructs through the zone of proximal development (ZPD). The ZPD was originally formulated by Vygotsky as "the distance between the actual developmental level as determined by independent problem solving and the level of potential development as determined through problem solving under adult guidance or in collaboration with more capable peers" (Vygotsky, 1978:86). According to Berk and Winsler (1995:24), Vygotsky argued that:

> [...] a child gets involved in a dialogue with the "knowledgeable other" such as a peer or an adult and gradually, through social interaction and sense-making, develops the ability to solve problems independently and do certain tasks without help. Following Vygotsky, some educators believe that the role of education is to give children experiences that are within their zones of proximal development, thereby encouraging and advancing their individual learning such as skills and strategies.

The ZPD is therefore the space in which the educator can assist the student, knowing their current level of knowledge and learning approach, and help them move further to acquire the knowledge and skills needed for the educational profession they are preparing for.

Understanding students and their 'demographics' is thus important for every educator. Students in the PGCE programme graduate from a range of faculties with different specialisation subjects. They thus have different needs, lived experiences and worldviews regarding teaching and learning in their field of expertise. Students also have different learning approaches, e.g. academic vs. non-academic students; those who learn through reading and writing, and those who learn visually or by doing. Students also come from various socio-economic backgrounds which adds to the variety of student goals and needs.

Defining educational demographics could be an empowering experience as this will allow myself as teacher educator to understand the cohort of pre-service teachers for the twenty-first century, and exactly what they want and need from teacher educators in the teaching and learning environment. Changing demographics should encourage educational institutions to rethink their academic offerings to include more diverse course content and delivery methods, in other words creating flexible learning environments or learning ecosystems that are capable of adapting to the changing teaching and learning aims and student profiles (Nasr & Ouf, 2011; Ouf, Nasr & Helmy, 2010).

In my years of being a teacher educator I have experienced many challenges specifically focused on the 'new generation', the twenty-first century generation, the millennials, Generation-Z or the iGeneration born between 1995 and 2009. More recently Generation-alpha (Gen-alpha) was described by Mark McCrindle (2014), a generational researcher and sociologist. Typically, the term Gen-alpha applies to children born between 2010 and 2025. They are truly the millennial generation, born and shaped fully in the twenty-first century. As Generation-Z (Gen-Z) began sitting their final school exams a year or so ago and then moving into tertiary education, the first Gen-alphas were beginning their schooling careers. A good understanding of these new generations is imperative as they are currently in the education system. Taking a closer look at the two generations currently in our schools and tertiary education institutions is a valuable exercise to determine the characteristics of this cohort of learners and students in our classrooms. Educational institutions will have to start thinking about new curricula, preparing flexible programmes to adapt and prepare according to the young Gen-alphas who are burning with curiosity, intrigued and extremely interested (Fourtané, 2018) in the modern advances and inventions of technology.

Generation-Z (Gen-Z)

My focus here will be on Gen-Z as this is the generation currently in secondary education and/or attending tertiary education. As educators we need to take cognisance of their characteristics and needs to promote effective learning. McCrindle (2014) identified seven factors that define Gen-Z. These are summarised below as characteristics to consider when preparing for teaching and learning for this student/learner cohort (Brotheim, 2014; McCrindle, 2014; Schneider Associates, 2014).

1. Demographically changed: Gen Z'ers are growing up in rapidly changing times. As a result they are emotionally driven and often rely on their emotions to make decisions.
2. Generationally defined: Gen-Z are the most materially endowed, technologically saturated, globally connected, formally educated generation our world has ever seen.
3. Digital integrators: Using technology from a very young age and seamlessly integrating technology into almost all areas of their lives, they are known as digital integrators and/or screenagers.

4. Globally focused: Gen-Z is the first generation to be truly global. Not only are music, movies and celebrities global for them as they have been for previous generations, but through technology, globalisation and our culturally diverse times, fashions, foods, online entertainment, social trends, communications and even 'must-watch' YouTube videos and memes are global as never before.
5. Visually engaged: Many students in this emerging generation will opt to watch videos summarising an issue rather than read an article discussing it. They often only participate in what they enjoy as they seek to cater for their personal qualities.
6. Educationally reformed: The average young person is spending more years in formal education than before, with tertiary education rates increasing. For today's students, education is no longer life-stage dependent but a life-long reality. They have a need for co-creating the curriculum to place their own stamp on learning. Learning style is mostly multi-modal and learner-centred; they would rather collaborate than work on their own.
7. Socially defined: More than any other generation, today's youth are extensively connected to and shaped by their peers. However, they often avoid uncomfortable situations or environments, looking for alternatives such as digital escapes. Effective marketing for Gen-Z would ideally be digital social media platforms such as Snapchat, iPhone, Twitter, and Instagram.

Technology is obviously a defining factor for the Gen-Z characteristics, making the Fourth Industrial Revolution (4IR) a reality in modern teaching and learning approaches. The question that researchers such as McCrindle (2014) ask is: How much more tech-intensive can the lives of Gen-alpha members possibly become? Gen-alpha is considered to have the most technologically infused demographic to date (Fourtané, 2018). This upcoming generation is truly the first millennial generation because they are the first generation born into the twenty-first century (Fourtané, 2018; McCrindle, 2014). They might just be the most influential generation of the twenty-first century, being exposed from a young age to digital devices (such as smartphones and tablets, iPhones and iPads) and phone applications that they use quite naturally as educational aids and entertainment tools (Fourtané, 2018; McCrindle, 2014). Gen-alphas, already at a very young age, are very direct and confident about expressing their opinions. They learn by doing. They are not afraid of technology and learn quite efficiently by pressing device buttons with confidence. They are likely to benefit from technology advancements such as Artificial Intelligence (AI), that are not only changing the world but also changing education. Interacting with AI and voice assistants such as 'Siri', 'Alexa' and 'Google Assistant' is simply natural in Gen-alpha households these days (Fourtané, 2018). This upcoming generation will not be able to fathom or imagine life without technology.

Following this understanding of the upcoming generations, it is also crucial to understand the future that young people face. As educators, we need to prepare them to face a yet unknown future (Butler-Adam, 2018).

The fourth industrial revolution

The first industrial revolution was known as the era of the steam engine and spanned 1760 to 1840. The second revolution that made mass production possible started in the late nineteenth century, and the third revolution, the computer era, began in the 1960s. The impact of the advancement of new technologies is profound, and thus the rise of the fourth industrial revolution (4IR) is inevitable (Schwab, 2016).

4IR is "characterized by a fusion of technologies that is blurring the lines between the physical, digital and biological spheres" (Schwab, 2016:7) bringing about societal transformation (Eiser, Mayet & Johnson, 2019). According to these authors 4IR simultaneously brings great opportunities and serious risks. Opportunities typically include new technologies that process information faster, drive economic growth and empower individuals, sparking entrepreneurship and improving the health system. At the same time, these new technologies pose serious risks, particularly from the perspectives of cybercrimes, leaked personal information, unemployment and inequality (Eiser et al., 2019; Schwab, 2016).

The world-renowned economist Klaus Schwab (2016:7), founder and executive chairman of the World Economic Forum, focuses on the opportunities and explains that: "We have an opportunity to shape the fourth industrial revolution, which will fundamentally alter how we live and work". This statement by Schwab poses challenges for society to understand and shape this new technological revolution, but what exactly is this revolution, and why does it matter, especially for [South] Africa? Technology is fast growing and the use of computers and mechanically operated devices (machines) are increasing day-by-day, doing the work that humans used to do. However, the human factor cannot be neglected in this industry, as human intelligence will always have an input in the advancement of technology. Schwab (2016:114) calls for leaders and citizens to:

> [...] together shape a future that works for all by putting people first, empowering them and constantly reminding ourselves that all of these new technologies are first and foremost tools made by people for people.

People in all communities need to acquire the skills to implement, manage and work with new technology, as well as becoming problem-solvers. New technologies can create new jobs, but technology can also nullify and replace existing jobs. A newfound need to upskill and re-skill employees to ensure they remain relevant in the workplace is important according to Eiser et al. (2019). Lifelong learning becomes essential for all, irrespective of age. This is especially important in light of Statistics South Africa's 2019 report on the high levels of unemployment in the country (Eiser et al., 2019; Statistics South Africa, 2019).

This challenge of upskilling and re-skilling is one to which educators will have to answer (Butler-Adam, 2018) as it has implications for teaching and learning, and more importantly for curriculum design and implementation. It is not only about AI and robotic tutors (Butler-Adam, 2018), but success as an informed citizen. Being an employee in the era of 4IR begs an understanding of how the world of technology operates. Johnson (in Eiser et al., 2019) makes it clear in his alarming statement that education in pre-school through to post-graduate education needs to be re-imagined. The education programme in SA must therefor incorporate emerging skills requirements with a particular emphasis placed on lifelong learning.

We, as educational practitioners in the twenty-first century, are therefore encouraged to re-curriculate educational curricula to adhere to the needs and wants of our pre-service teachers. Training is needed to secure competent newly qualified teachers for the future and simultaneously encourage life-long learning. The burning question of previous centuries remains: What knowledge is of most worth? Since the beginning of formal schooling, this famous question has kept educators occupied in pondering what knowledge [and curricula] are of most value.

Harvey (2017), a senior researcher in Natural Resource Governance (Africa) at the South African Institute of International Affairs, argues that policymakers, academics and companies must understand why all these advances matter and what should be done about them. He believes that AI and 3-D printing pose further challenges for industry and education, and asks the question: How do we prepare our young people of today for this future? The answer lies in "technologically informed pedagogic practices" that bring about informed, responsible and life-long learning citizens (Waghid, Waghid & Waghid, 2019:4), who expand their technological knowledge and skill-sets in preparation for the demands of 4IR and the twenty-first century curriculum.

Policy

Teacher education policies have been reformulated, as set out in the Government Gazette of 19 February 2015 (DHET, 2015), and are currently being, or have already been, implemented by various national higher education institutions. This reformulation involves the rethinking and restructuring of teacher education programmes such as the Postgraduate Certificate in Education (PGCE) and the Bachelor of Education (BEd) degree in either the Foundation, Intermediate or Senior Phases. Adaptations must align with the national qualifications framework developed by the Department of Higher Education and Training (DHET) including a policy on *Minimum Requirements for Teacher Education Qualifications* (MRTEQ) (DHET, 2015:8).

According to this policy, the PGCE programme has a primary purpose of offering entry-level, initial professional preparation for undergraduate degree/diploma holders who wish to develop focused knowledge and skills as classroom teachers. Together with specialisation knowledge, practical skills and workplace experience in varying contexts, it needs to provide a well-rounded education that equips graduates with the required educational theory and methodology to demonstrate competence and responsibility as academically and professionally qualified beginner teachers. A set of minimum competences are required of newly qualified teachers as set out in Appendix C of the MRTEQ document (DHET, 2015:62). These competences correlate with the institutional graduate attributes (Stellenbosch University, 2012) (Table 4.1) that endeavour to provide knowledgeable, critically engaged, responsible, life-long learners as informed and competent leaders and citizens in their communities. It is therefore envisaged to equip beginner teachers to make a positive impact in improving the quality of education in our country.

The new PGCE programme at Stellenbosch University is underpinned by Productive Pedagogies, a framework for reflecting on teaching and learning that aims at improving students' intellectual reasoning and that makes teaching and learning more connected to a student's everyday life. The framework also addresses concerns about equity and student support (Lingard, Hayes & Mills, 2003). It affords educators the opportunity to invest in the different types of knowledge that underpin teaching and teaching practices, and the theory and practice. Critical thinking becomes of the utmost importance while encapsulating all the knowledge, skills and competences in the notion of integrated/mixed and applied knowledge.

Table 4.1 Institutional graduate attributes related to novice teacher competence

INSTITUTIONAL GRADUATE ATTRIBUTES (Stellenbosch University, 2012)	NEWLY QUALIFIED TEACHERS' COMPETENCE (DHET, 2015:62)
Have a sound subject knowledge base	… must have sound subject knowledge
Demonstrate the ability to think and reflect critically	… must know how to teach their subject(s) and how to select the content in accordance with both subject and learner needs
Have a holistic worldview	… must know who their learners are and how they learn; they must understand their individual needs and tailor their teaching accordingly
Demonstrate the ability to function optimally in a team context	… must know how to communicate effectively in general, as well as in relation to their subject(s), in order to mediate learning
Demonstrate responsible citizenship (active citizenship)	… must have highly developed literacy, numeracy and Information Technology (IT) skills
Demonstrate an appreciation for diversity (in its broadest sense) and make a contribution towards the development of these contexts	… must be knowledgeable about the school curriculum and be able to unpack its specialised content
Demonstrate leadership	… must understand diversity in the South African context in order to teach in a manner that includes all learners
Have a commitment towards life-long learning	… must be able to manage classrooms effectively across diverse contexts in order to ensure a conducive learning environment
Take the responsibility to make a contribution towards the development of human potential	… must be able to assess learners in reliable and varied ways, as well as being able to use the results of assessment to improve teaching and learning
	… must have a positive work ethic, reflect critically on their own practice, in theoretically informed ways

Criticality or critical thinking is one of the most desirable and important core outcomes of higher education (Facione, 1990; Lederer, 2007:525) in order for students to acquire deep knowledge and an understanding of the curriculum with which they engage. Critical thinking has also been described as the essence of education (Facione, 1990) and has a central role in teaching and learning (McPeck, 1981).

At tertiary level, critical thinking is essential to meet assessment criteria (Elander, Harrington, Norton, Robinson & Reddy, 2006). It is also associated with employability and academic achievement of graduating students (Halx & Reybold, 2005). Dwyer, Hogan and Stewart (2014) suggest that graduates with critical thinking skills have enhanced ability to draw sound conclusions and make informed decisions, which enhances innovation in the workplace and society (Davies, 2006). However, many students struggle to understand critical thinking. They lack confidence in being critical; are unsure of how to develop critical thinking skills and struggle to demonstrate criticality in their assessments (Elander et al., 2006).
Critical thinking is complex and not easily defined. Facione (1990:3) alludes to expert consensus from the American Philosophical Associations' committee on Pre-College Philosophy that defined critical thinking as: "Purposeful, self-regulatory judgment which results in interpretation, analysis, evaluation, and inference, as well as explanation of the evidential, conceptual, methodological, criteriological, or contextual considerations upon which that judgment is based". This definition captures the "complex, multifaceted nature of critical thinking", which may explain the difficulties students have with understanding the concept and principle of being critical (Facione, 1990:2).

The core challenge, therefore, is to develop a flexible curriculum that addresses the question of what knowledge and pedagogies are of most worth. At the same time, the needs of new generation students must be considered within the policy framework so that critical thinkers graduate from the system. Such a curriculum should be informed by appropriate philosophies, policy and the underpinning framework in order to support good teaching and learning that facilitate local adaptations and ownership of the curriculum (Barab & Luehmann, 2003). Taking ownership of teaching and learning to educate for enhanced learning becomes imperative. Ownership of teaching and learning means becoming a scholar of teaching and learning who can address the myriad of expectations of an appropriate curriculum and necessary change.

What are the challenges for the Curriculum Studies module?

All three philosophers, Dewey, Piaget and Vygotsky, emphasised that students do not come to class as blank canvases: they all have prior knowledge and lived experiences. Students must be afforded opportunities to blend prior knowledge with new knowledge and experiences through collaboration with peers and older adult experts. In this way, a student will be able to progress from individual learning to collaborative learning.

Although an attempt has been made to follow a student-centred, constructivist approach according to early twentieth century philosophers, it seems that students are still struggling to engage with subject content and thus not critically engaged in their own teaching and learning. Implementing the new PGCE programme necessitates a fresh take on the presentation of the Curriculum Studies module, as this module forms a core component in initial teacher education and training comprising current educational debates on curriculum design and development. The teaching and learning activities (TLAs) include student readings from relevant literature, lecture sessions, interactive class discussions where critical debate is encouraged, assignments and formal tests.

Specific topics related to curriculum in the South African context were shared amongst three staff members, each an expert in his/her own field. To break the cycle of a traditional way of teaching, the colleagues collaborated in creating critical engagement opportunities to assist students in understanding a variety of current curriculum debates. These topics include:

- Contemporary curriculum theories and their influence on teaching and learning.
- What is curriculum? – including the perennial question: What knowledge is of most worth?
- Why is the curriculum such a contentious subject?
- Why is curriculum change so difficult?
- What does government expect from teachers with respect to the curriculum?
- How do you know the curriculum made a difference?
- What do creative teachers do with a prescribed curriculum?
- Curriculum design, development and implementation.
- Teacher involvement in curriculum development/curriculum agents.
- Teaching strategies/methods.

Initially the TLAs seemed equally do-able and/or difficult, but assessment results indicated a very different outcome. Anecdotal evidence based on personal experiences in the classroom and through assessing assignments and tests, alluded to student teachers' lack of criticality. They struggled to critically engage with literature provided and to apply it as problem-solvers to current and burning curriculum debates. This was evident from the non-interactive class discussions that resulted from pre-service teachers being unprepared for these lectures. They did not engage with the literature prior to the lectures, failing to give a valid representation of their [supposedly] learned knowledge. Individual tasks and group assignments showed a lack of critical thinking as student teachers did not incorporate their own views and experiences linked to the readings provided for the assessment tasks. Answers given in assessment tasks were superficial and simple with little evidence of deep and critical engagement with the content. Students are not involved in dialogue with the "knowledgeable other" (Vygotsky, 1978:86), the educator. In the current social environment of learning where we deal with large numbers of students, they should be able to develop the ability to critically engage with curriculum issues and solve problems independently. I was therefore not able to present the course that I had planned as it became clear that my perceptions are different from those of the students, and this gap can be hard to overcome (Audley, 2018). Assisting students to move forward in their own understanding of curriculum and curriculum debates during lectures, and advancing their individual learning, becomes a challenging task. Audley (2018) is of the opinion that student pedagogical partners can provide unique scaffolding to assist educators to teach in ways that are in line with our students' experiences and needs.

So, what does this tell us about our scholarship of teaching and learning? Is our teaching practice conducive to the training of an effective new generation of teachers for the new decade/millennium and the unknown future? These questions point to a need to re-imagine the current teaching and learning taking place in the Curriculum Studies module. Re-imagining curriculum necessarily brings about changes to the curriculum design and development. This therefore necessitates the lecturer or facilitator becoming an agent of curriculum change, and becoming a scholar of teaching and learning. Change is not easy or merely accepted (Audley, 2018; Miller-Young et al., 2017) as humans resist change in many instances. Therefore leadership is crucial in changing the direction of teaching and learning for future generations. As a leader and scholar of teaching and learning, I need to review current practices by critically challenging and transforming perceptions and [world] view on what effective and excellent teaching encompass.

Being a change agent means to make a difference in the training provided for the new generation, the new teachers of the future. These changes need to inform continuing professional development, not only for students but also for educators. Investing in a scholarship of teaching and learning could ensure effective changes take place (Miller-Young et al., 2017) and, in turn, inform good teaching that narrows the gap between the differences, that is, in the various learning styles/strategies, demographics and needs of students (Biggs, 2012). Drawing on Lewin's (1952) model of change, it becomes clear that certain worldviews need to be changed: *unfreeze*, *change* and then *re-freeze*. Some learned perceptions need to be deconstructed (unfreeze) before an intervention with new sets of knowledge, skills and pedagogies, and thus change, can be attempted. Opportunity arises within every new lecture and every new student to make a change drawing on in-course and out-of-course experiences (Quinn et al., 2012). In-course changes could be afforded by means of collaboration: between colleagues (also from other higher education institutions) and students. Out-of-course changes could draw on prior knowledge and experiences/expertise from both educators and students/learners.

Now that a critical understanding of the future generation and current student cohort has been established, the challenge of change needs to be addressed. There is a dire need to identify what subject content/knowledge is of most worth. What is most relevant and conducive to student learning? Scholarship of teaching and learning seems key as it leads to effective change and affords capacity to influence others [educators and students] to work towards a common goal or set of goals (Miller-Young et al., 2017). Becoming a scholar means to be a leader; a leader who can provide the necessary tools for successful change to occur. A leader in curriculum change, pedagogy and methods can adapt his/her subject curriculum to address the needs of diverse students in the classroom. Change can happen in any context and at any level. It can occur in any classroom, lecture, educational institution, grade, study year or post level. It depends on a leader in the field critically considering new ways of thinking, doing and engaging with teaching and learning. To make these changes happen and stick (freeze) a good leader should weave the value of teaching and learning scholarship into the educational institution by applying leadership activities and actions to advance teaching and learning (Miller-Young et al., 2017).

In addition to corporate leaders, educators, schools, government officials and parents must re-think education and how to prepare the next generation to overcome the challenges enabled by ever-increasing technological change (Marr, 2019). Primary schools, secondary schools and tertiary institutions of education need to consider how to adjust to the new world, the 4IR, as learners and students will need to be educated very differently than in the past decades. According to Marr (2019), technologies are disrupting every industry across the world at unprecedented speed, and some of the changes already happening include automation, AI, big data, augmented reality and the Internet. Marr (2019) argues that young people need to be prepared to engage in a world alongside smart machines, and suggests eight domains of action to address the challenge of preparing for the future and for careers still unknown. Marr's[1] (2019) domains are summarised below and include:

- The purpose of education needs to be redefined in order to support students in developing knowledge and skillsets that enable them to do basically everything in future.
- Improving science, technology, engineering and mathematics (STEM) education across various disciplines as everyone will need to be technically skilled, and have an understanding of the values and ethics of the new technology they engage with.
- Education systems should assist in the development of human potential, e.g. creativity, imagination, critical thinking, social interaction and physical dexterity, so that they are equipped to work alongside the machine rather than compete with it.
- Education should become a lifelong endeavour to prepare for the yet unknown future in 4IR, thus continuing with structured education beyond school or tertiary education.
- Re-think teacher education and training to support teachers in becoming facilitators, assisting students to facilitate their own learning and lines of inquiry that include technologies such as AI and robotics.
- Adapting undergraduate and postgraduate qualifications to become more focused on 4IR, affording students the opportunity to learn topics beyond their core curriculum.
- Providing learning spaces in education that will enable students to be creators of their own learning, to practice their curiosity and problem-solving skills, and help them make sense of their lived world through hands-on experiences.
- Teaching and learning philosophies of educators and educational institutions need to be reconsidered to take into account the need of international demands such as the languages of emerging markets in 4IR.

Dewey[2] said that: "If we teach today's students as we taught yesterday's, we rob them of tomorrow". I concur and strongly believe that these areas of action can be beneficial in preparing tertiary education students for tomorrow, the technological age.

---

1   Marr (2019) at https://bit.ly/3n9GIqK
2   John Dewey Quotes at https://bit.ly/36i3Uwn

Conclusion

After considering the various levels of knowledge needed for effective and efficient teaching and learning in an attempt to answer the perennial curriculum question – What knowledge is of most worth for future generations in the new millennium? – there is clearly an argument to invest in the scholarship of teaching and learning to bring about much needed change in curriculum.

In our rapidly developing technological age where the Internet, virtual reality and AI change daily life, it becomes crucial to revisit the teaching and learning (curriculum) of teacher education, not only in schools but also at the level of higher education. It is also true that to develop curriculum, consideration should be given to existing praxis. Students and educators, and universities and schools, need to develop specific qualities, skills and understanding regarding their disciplines and beyond in order to prepare the new generations as "agents of social good in an unknown future" (Bowden et al., 2000:1). GenZ and Gen-alpha are the first generations to spend their entire adolescence in the age of technology and in the social media domain where they construct their own knowledge about knowledge and education.

To summarise the discussion in this chapter regarding the new generation, new millennium and what curriculum is of most worth in these times, the following keys concepts were highlighted. The twentieth century philosophers Dewey, Piaget and Vygotsky refer to learning through experience and prior knowledge, social interactions, adult guidance and collaboration. Students follow stages of development to construct their own learning through problem-solving skills, problem-based and inquiry-based learning with the necessary support from the educator. The graduate attributes and novice teacher competences strongly point to the development of human potential through team-work [collaboration], communication and leadership, in order to become responsible, literate and skilled citizens, culminating in the notion of life-long learning, one of the collective roles of an educator (DHET, 2015). The framework of Productive Pedagogies strongly invests in critical thinking and criticality, deep knowledge and intellectual quality, connectedness to curriculum, active citizenship, academic engagement and self-regulation. Marr's eight domains for action (2019) strongly relate to most, if not all, of the requirements needed to be considered for curriculum change in preparation for the future. These include the development of new mind-sets where human curiosity and creativity culminate in construction of their own learning. They learn about topics beyond the core, acquiring new skills such as critical thinking skills to solve problems, and collaboration and interaction with a variety of intelligences. Individuals need to be able to unlearn [unfreeze], change/intervene and re-learn [refreeze] to become the life-long learners needed to progress into an unknown future.

"Education is our passport to the future, for tomorrow belongs to the people who prepare for it today" (anon). As educators, it is our responsibility to work towards an improved curriculum and educational system (Beierling, 2014) as "we cannot expect to meaningfully participate in the transformation of the nation and its educational institutions if we fail to authentically participate in the constitution and transformation of ourselves and our work" (Pinar, 1994:74 in Beierling, 2014).

The *Method of Currere* (Pinar, 1975) is fundamental for understanding the meaning of curriculum development. The meaning of *currere*, to 'run the racecourse', is still relevant for scholars and educators of curriculum entering the twenty-first century. Its transformational work empowers us with the agency and the momentum required to bring about much needed transformation for modern teaching and learning (Beierling, 2014). As curriculum change agents and scholars of teaching and learning in the twenty-first century embarking on preparing the new generation for an unknown future, it might become possible to establish what knowledge is of most worth if we engage with, and revisit the notion of currere, to run the modern race.

References

Audley, S. 2018. Partners as scaffolds: Teaching in the Zone of Proximal Development. *Teaching and learning together in higher education*, 24(4):1-5. Available online: https://bit.ly/2Ii0oKs [accessed 8 May 2020].

Barab, S. & Luehmann, A. 2003. Building sustainable science curriculum: Acknowledging and accommodating local adaptation. *Science Education*, 87:454-467. https://doi.org/10.1002/sce.10083

Beierling, S. 2014. "Course" Work: Pinar's Currere as an initiation into Curriculum Studies. *Canadian Journal for New Scholars in Education*, 5(2):1-9.

Berk, L. & Winsler, A. 1995. *Vygotsky's approach to development. Scaffolding children's learning: Vygotsky and early childhood learning*. Washington, DC: National Association for the Education of Young Children.

Biggs, J. 2012. What the student teacher does: Teaching for enhanced learning. *Higher Education Research and Development*, 31(1):39-55. https://doi.org/10.1080/07294360.2012.642839

Bowden, J., Hart, G., King, B., Trigwell, K. & Watts, O. 2000. Generic capabilities of ATN university graduates. Canberra: Australian Government Department of Education, Training and Youth Affairs. Available online: https://bit.ly/2InbgXi [accessed 8 May 2020]

Brotheim, H. 2014. Introducing Generation Z. *American Jails*, 28(5):15.

Broudy, H.S. 1982. What knowledge is of most worth? *Educational Leadership* 39(8):574-578. Available online: https://bit.ly/32rr0jc [accessed 20 November 2019].

Butler-Adam J. 2018. The fourth industrial revolution and education. *South African Journal of Science*, 114 (5/6):1. https://doi.org/10.17159/sajs.2018/a0271

Carey, S., Zaitchik, D. & Bascandziev, I. 2015. Theories of development: In dialog with Jean Piaget. *Developmental Review*, 38:36-54. https://doi.org/10.1016/j.dr.2015.07.003

Davies, T. 2006. Creative teaching and learning in Europe: Promoting a new paradigm. *The Curriculum Journal*, 17(1):37-57. https://doi.org/10.1080/09585170600682574

DHET (Department of Higher Education and Training). 2015. *Revised policy on the minimum requirements for teacher education qualifications*. Government Gazette No 38487. Pretoria, South Africa: Department of Higher Education and Training.

Dewey, J. 1938. *Experience & Education*. New York, NY: Kappa Delta Pi.

Dwyer, C.P., Hogan, M.J. & Stewart, I. 2014. An integrated critical thinking framework for the 21st century. *Thinking Skills and Creativity*, 12:43-52. https://doi.org/10.1016/j.tsc.2013.12.004

Eiser, K., Mayet, I. & Johnson, S. 2019. 4IR and the South African workplace. Business Technology Media Company. Issued by Webber Wentzel, Johannesburg, 14 Aug. Available online: https://bit.ly/36j3Ind [accessed 31 Juanuary 2020].

Elander, J., Harrington, K., Norton, L., Robinson, H. & Reddy, P. 2006. Complex skills and academic writing: A review of evidence about the types of learning required to meet core assessment criteria. *Assessment & Evaluation in Higher Education*, 31(1):71-90. https://doi.org/10.1080/02602930500262379

Facione, P.A. 1990. *Critical thinking: A statement of expert consensus for purposes of educational assessment and instruction.* Millbrae, CA: California Academic Press.

Felicia, P. (Ed). 2011. Handbook of research on improving learning and motivation. IGI Global. USA. https://doi.org/10.4018/978-1-60960-495-0

Fourtané, S. 2018. *Generation Alpha: The children of the millennial.* Available online: https://bit.ly/3kh2V4u [accessed 8 May 2020].

Halx, M.D. & Reybold, L.E. 2005. A pedagogy of force: Faculty perspectives of critical thinking capacity in undergraduate students. *Journal of General Education*, 54:293-315. https://doi.org/10.1353/jge.2006.0009

Harvey, R. 2017. The 'fourth industrial revolution': Potential and risks for Africa. *The Conversation*. Available online: https://bit.ly/2JRrG13 [accessed 20 November 2019].

Henson, K. 2003. Foundations for learner-centered education: A knowledge base. *Education*, 124(1):5-16.

Hodgkinson, H. 2001. The changing context of education. *Educational Leadership*. 58(4):6-11.

Huitt, W. & Hummel, J. 2003. Piaget's theory of cognitive development. Educational Psychology Interactive. Valdosta, GA: Valdosta State University. Available online: https://bit.ly/2IixuKd [accessed 6 May 2020].

Lederer, J.M. 2007. Disposition towards critical thinking among occupational therapy students. *American Journal of Occupational Therapy*, 61:519-526. https://doi.org/10.5014/ajot.61.5.519

Lewin, K. 1952. Group decision and social change. In: G.E. Swanson, T.M. Newcomb & E.L. Hartley (eds), *Readings in social psychology.* New York: Holt, Reinhart and Winston, pp. 459-473.

Lingard, B., Hayes, D. & Mills, M. 2003. Teachers and Productive Pedagogies: Contextualising, conceptualising, utilising. *Pedagogy, culture and society*. 11(3):399-424. https://doi.org/10.1080/14681360300200181

Marr, B. 2019. 8 Things every school must do to prepare for the 4th Industrial Revolution, May 22. Forbes Media. Available online: https://bit.ly/3n9GIqK [accessed 8 Feb 2020].

McCrindle, M. 2014. *The ABC of XYZ: Understanding the Global Generations.* McCrindle Research.

McPeck, J.E. 1981. Critical thinking in education. *Philosophy of Education*, 12. Routledge, Taylor & Francis Group. London and New York.

Miller-Young, J.E., Anderson, C., Kiceniuk, D., Mooney, J., Riddell, J., Schmidt Hanbidge, A., Ward, V., Wideman, M.A. & Chick, N. 2017. Leading up in the scholarship of teaching and learning. *The Canadian Journal for the Scholarship of Teaching and Learning*, 8(2), Article 4:1-18. https://doi.org/10.5206/cjsotl-rcacea.2017.2.4

Nasr, M. & Ouf, S. 2011. An ecosystem in e-Learning using cloud computing as platform and Web2.0. *The Research Bulletin of Jordan ACM*, II (IV):134-140.

Ouf, S., Nasr, M. & Helmy, Y. 2010. An enhanced e-learning ecosystem based on an integration between cloud computing and Web 2.0. The 10th IEEE International Symposium on Signal Processing and Information Technology [Conference proceedings]. https://doi.org/10.1109/ISSPIT.2010.5711721

Piaget, J. 1971. *Psychology and epistemology: Towards a theory of knowledge.* New York: Grossman.

Pinar, W. 1975. The method of "currere". Paper presented at the annual meeting of the American Research Association, Washington D.C.

Quinn, D., Amer, Y. & Lonie, A. 2012. Leading change: Applying change management approaches to engage students in blended learning. *Australasian Journal of Educational Technology*, 28(1):1-29. https://doi.org/10.14742/ajet.881

Rolfe, G., Freshwater, D. & Jasper, M. 2001. *Critical reflection in nursing and the helping professions: A user's guide.* Basingstoke: Palgrave Macmillan.

Schneider Associates. 2014. *BG's "iGen Goes to School" study reveals class of 2020 wants personalized communications during college enrolment.* Available online: https://bit.ly/3l8fkZP [accessed 10 Augustus 2019].

Seifert, K. & Sutton, R. 2009. *Educational Psychology*. 2nd Edition. Available online: https://bit.ly/3lgQrvc [accessed 28 January 2020].

Schwab, K. 2016. *The fourth industrial revolution.* Cologny: World Economic Forum.

Statistics South Africa. 2019. *Quarterly Labour Force Survey: Quarter 1* (January to March 2019). Available online: https://bit.ly/3eGNZLP [accessed 8 May 2020].

Stellenbosch University. 2012. *Graduate attributes.* Available online: https://bit.ly/3eH4ozS [accessed 28 January 2020].

The Tambellini Group. 2018. Available online: https://bit.ly/3k6ppFm [accessed 6 December 2019].

Vygotsky, L.S. 1978. *Mind in society: The development of higher psychological processes.* In: M. Cole, V. John-Steiner, S. Scribner, & E. Souberman (eds), Cambridge, MA: Harvard University Press.

Waghid, Y., Waghid, Z. & Waghid, F. 2019. The fourth industrial revolution reconsidered: On advancing cosmopolitan education. *South African Journal of Higher Education* 33(6): 1-9. https://doi.org/10.20853/33-6-3777

5

Auto-ethnographic reflections on an Education Governance, Leadership and Management module

Jerome Joorst

Introduction

Education is currently framed by neoliberal regulatory impulses, which form part of broader, macro-economic discourses in the world. These discourses are more and more characterised by quantitative, technological demands on students and teachers (Jones, 2019; Lingard, 2011; Maistry, 2014). Characterised by artificial intelligence, big data, mobile internet, cloud technology, drones, and driverless vehicles (World Economic Forum, 2016), the fourth industrial revolution's (4IR) imperatives not only disrupt our normative thinking of humans' interaction with machines, but also the relationship between schooling and the kinds of skills needed for the labour market of the twenty-first century. In schools, teachers and learners are overburdened with assessment tasks and asked to follow tightly prescribed curriculum scripts mechanistically. Universities, in turn, are expected to produce readymade teachers who can fit smoothly and uncritically into these regulated environments.

What complicates matters is that despite many positive changes apartheid realities still haunt education in South Africa. Most schools in South Africa are still underperforming by regional and international standards (Howie et al., 2017; Spaull, 2018). Former racialised segregation has now changed to economic segregation. A history of colonialism, the effects of migrant labour and the implementation of the Group Areas Act in 1950, forcibly located black people on the outskirts of cities or towns. The legacy of this 'separate development' system (Schoeman, 2018) is still very noticeable in the contrasts between spacious, leafy areas where white people predominantly reside, with dusty, cramped low cost housing or informal settlements where mostly black South Africans live. Not only does South Africa have among the highest levels of income inequality in the world, but this inequality is still strongly racialised in nature. Former whites-only schools still have far more resources, better-trained teachers and bigger budgets due to well-off parents and support from white-owned businesses.

While there is some movement in trying to diversify, it is still very much only the relatively small group of elite black families who can afford to move into former Model C and private schools. The vast majority of children still have substandard schools in terms of infrastructure, teacher qualifications, parental support and corporate sponsorship. Spaull refers to this as the "two-tier education system" (2013:26). Newly graduated teachers often do not want to teach in the bottom tier schools. Adding to the challenges, many teachers currently in the system are either unqualified or underqualified, especially in rural areas (Jansen, 2012).

Currently a professionally qualified teacher in South Africa should have a Relative Education Qualification Value (REQV) of level 14. A Postgraduate Certificate in Education (PGCE) provides teachers with such a professional qualification. The Faculty of Education at Stellenbosch University offers the PGCE programme to students who have already obtained a Bachelor's degree. This is based on a perception that such students already have the necessary subject content knowledge. A professional qualification is aimed at equipping student teachers with the knowledge, skills and disposition attributes that they need to teach the disciplinary knowledge to children in schools. This assumes that university (propositional) knowledge, combined with practical (micro-teaching and teaching practice) knowledge will, according to the Stellenbosch University (2012) graduate attributes, produce teachers with enquiring minds who become not only engaged and dynamic professionals, but also well-rounded citizens.

The current demands of what good teachers should look like are complex. Coupled with the country's histories and current education realities characterised by the continuing two-tiered system, heavy demands rest on teacher education. The PGCE curriculum consists of three main parts, namely: core education modules, teaching specialisation modules and teaching practice. The core modules introduce students to key propositional knowledge about curriculum, history of education, diversity and inclusivity, education policies, leadership and management, sociology and philosophy of education and theories of education. The specialisation modules focus on the teaching of particular school subjects and the pedagogical content knowledge of a particular subject. The teaching practice component focuses on practical teaching (in controlled micro-teaching environments or in schools for a term).

In this chapter, I examine the contextual, institutional and personal complexities I faced in the design and teaching of a module in the PGCE programme – Education Governance, Leadership and Management – and what I learnt from it. All of the broad issues mentioned above come to bear in the daily, lived experience of being a teacher educator in South Africa, including this university's institutional culture, what is expected to be taught in this module, the identities of the students and how non-traditional academics in this university do their teaching.

Who am I in relation to the research?

I was born and raised in a poor family in the Boland area of the Western Cape province in South Africa at a time where people, neighbourhoods and schools were still racially classified as so-called coloured.[1] I was socialised in coloured communities, attended schools and received most of my tertiary education at education institutions designated for coloured people. As a teacher and researcher, I often reflect on my interaction with the world. I believe that our experiences with the world have an impact on our future engagements with the world. Our lived experiences in the world, I believe, shape our realities.

---

1   Disclaimer: I use the term, 'coloured' in this chapter reluctantly and only as a forced, political identity as I believe racial categories in South Africa are socially constructed and were historically used as tools to 'other' and dehumanize through legislation. Race classifications find their genesis in European colonial, imperialist, white supremacist structuring of the world that wanted to use false science to justify their expansionist rhetoric as well as their inhumane treatment of fellow human beings. 'Coloured' is a term that stems from this false categorisation, 'homo monstrous', meaning abnormal or subhuman. 'Hotentots' or 'Hotnots' is the derogatory, white supremacist apartheid version that stems from the same false science of Carl Linneaus (1735 in Kwah Prah, 2002). I therefore use this term in this chapter to express the hurtful knowledge in my blood.

Where did I gain these beliefs?

My understanding of the self has been informed by my sociological engagements throughout my life. Berger and Luckmann (1966) argued that society is created by humans and human interactions in a process called habitualisation. Habitualisation describes how: "... any action that is repeated frequently becomes cast into a pattern, which can be ... performed again in the future in the same manner and with the same economical effort" (Berger & Luckmann, 1966:43). Spiritually, I believe that all human beings are made in the image of God, meaning that we are all equal before God and that all humans have inherent dignity and significance. In his book, *Outline of a theory of practice*, Bourdieu notes that:

> ... every established order tends to produce (to very different degrees and with very different means) the naturalization of its own arbitrariness. This is produced by the objective structures in our society and the subjective agency in individuals ... [called] our 'sense of reality.' (Bourdieu & Passeron, 1977:164)

Following Bourdieu, I believe that our social principles, worldview and sense of reality are socially constructed by the connections between mental and social structures, which become normalised over time. I also believe that cultural differences between individuals exist as a result of their habitus (how a person was socialised – social class, ethnicity, tastes, attributes); fields (social context into which an individual's habitus enters, like the fields of arts, politics, law) which Bourdieu believed were structured by the middle and upper classes in French society); and, cultural capitals (something that everyone has, determined by the sum of the individual's habitus and the field in which they entered).

How do these beliefs influence the way I react to situations or people?

Although I embrace the idea of democratic citizenship and everything that accompanies it, I am also keen on persistent forms of symbolic violence in South African society broadly and in South African schools and university lecture halls specifically. I am therefore keenly focused on the idea of socially just pedagogies as a way of addressing continued discriminatory practices in education. I will therefore focus on content that interrogates notions of social injustice in education and take (through my teaching, research and social impact engagements) a firm stance against social injustices. I am, however, aware that I may have blind spots. According to Mezirow, critical reflection allows us to undertake a process of making a new or revised interpretation of the meaning of an experience, which underpins further interpretation in future experiences (1990:6). As Chang (2008) argues, "autoethnography helps one to, not only critically reflect on the cultural understanding of the self and others, but that it also has the potential to transform self and others toward the cross-cultural coalition building" (213).

I was trained as a high school teacher but taught in high- and primary schools designated for coloured people in rural communities allocated for coloured people. After being a schoolteacher/manager for 20 years, I joined this university as a junior lecturer in the Faculty of Education. As a teacher educator, I was now located in a post-racial Faculty of Education in a former whites-only, Afrikaans university. Despite national reform regulations, and against the background of particularly precarious race relations between Europeans, indigenous people and indentured slaves, my university struggled to make its institutional culture relevant to multi-diverse race groups in South Africa. When I joined the university, both it and the school communities in the province were still reeling from incidents of racial conflict. I taught a module entitled 'Perspectives of Education Systems' to fourth year Bachelor of Education (Foundation/Intermediate, and Senior Phase) students. I also taught students who came from diverse undergraduate studies and now wanted to do education in a module called 'Education Governance, Leadership and Management' (Stellenbosch University, 2012). I 'inherited' these modules as part of the restructuring of a post vacated by a senior academic, which I now occupy.

The expectations and set outcomes of this module included an understanding of and application of school governance, management and leadership issues in practice. However, they were based on set notions of what school governance, management and leadership entailed and came across as a normative blueprint on these aspects of education. While some aspects of the module seemed applicable to me, from my experience it also appeared somewhat disconnected from the lived realities of minority students in the class – something I was used to as a former teacher in previously underserved schools. As I started teaching the module, I soon realised that my students (most of whom were white females) had very different assumptions and views of a teacher and schools to my own. I also noted that my beliefs and knowledge of the purpose of education in general, and the role of a teacher specifically, were being challenged. Some of my students challenged me in class while others disengaged from class discussions or activities. It often felt as if I was teaching diverse, multicultural classes in a neo-racial lecture hall.

In class, as well as on evaluation forms, my (mostly white) students expressed opposition to what I teach. This, added to my positionality as a minority in an institution with a white, male-dominated culture, made me start doubting the relevance of my teaching content as well as teaching strategies. My hopes for a socially just society in which education plays a critical role led me to want to understand how I could invite robust, courageous conversations about education governance, leadership and management issues in a diverse society, in a safe, congenial and controlled lecture room. I align myself with Fraser's (2009) notion of robust justice in conditions of the present-becoming-future. This is a kind of justice:

> ... that is inclusive and egalitarian in terms of: (a) redistributing material and cultural resources needed for good lives; (b) recognising cultural histories and practices of diverse groups in the institutional formations within which they are subjected; and (c) participatory-democratic representing of diverse social groups in processes that define and enact the ways, means and norms for 'a good life.' (Zipin, 2017:68)

Drawing on Freire's *Pedagogy of the Oppressed* and his later *Pedagogy of Hope* (2006 in Botman, 2007; Le Grange, 2011), I began to rethink the pedagogies that would create a space for students to engage in conversations about the role of novice educators in a university through disrupting divisive narratives. I also drew inspiration for my role as a lecturer from Vygotsky's (1978) concept of the educator playing a mediating or scaffolding role in the gap between what students already know and what they need assistance to learn. For Vygotsky learning takes place at the social level. I drew on his work to address how to set up the social conditions in the university classroom.

South African educators' identities have been affected by race-based policies in the past that have created fragmented populations that still exist in the democratic dispensation. Singh (1997:120) argues that apartheid acted as "a powerful allocator of identity" and frequently "suppressed identity through centralizing [sic] race and ethnicity at the expense of other markers of identity". Since the dawn of South African democracy, however, dramatic sociocultural changes have occurred in South Africa (Moloi & Henning, 2006) that now require different groups formerly categorised racially to forge new identities and positioning in society. This, Francis and Le Roux (2011) argue, has resulted in the resurgence of issues of identity. As educators, I believe we have to co-construct with learners a new language that can reshape new identities, to fashion new understandings of who we are and who we can be as democratic citizens. If educators are expected to understand and mediate diversity in schools, they need to engage with such issues personally at university level.

However, we live in a world in which social-structural inequalities of power and wellbeing are intensifying, making ethically informed, transformative curriculum and pedagogy even more important. I favour the notion of a transformative curriculum that is informed by an ethical impulse of "pursuing what is worth working towards" (Zipin, 2017:77), questioning the social realist-informed national curriculum which yields nothing other than a conservation of coded grammars which continue to reproduce power inequalities (Bourdieu & Passeron, 1990).

Methodology

The aim of this chapter is to reflect, not just for the sake of reflection, but to critically look at what Zeichner and Liston (2014:35) call "the particular and more subtle features" of reflection. I do this to understand my thinking and practices and their effects with the aim of improvement. Teacherly reflection as an inquiry-based learning practice finds its roots in the ideas of, amongst others, Kolb's (1984) experiential learning cycles, Schön's (1987) reflection in and on action, and Dewey's (1933) reflective thinking. Reflection is useful because it provides me with points of reference against which I can judge my pitch of a pedagogy of social justice which, in the words of Postma (2016:312), "aims to develop an ethical subjectivity that could resist and overcome neoliberal subjectification". For Strom and Martin (2013), a pedagogy of social justice is an ongoing process of self-reflection on the effects of pedagogical practices. To them, the classroom is "a site of perpetual transformation" of both educators and students who connect with their histories, local communities, course materials and policies (Strom & Martin, 2013: 226).

Zeichner (2007) notes that: "Self-study research can make an important contribution to teacher education throughout the world in that it can add dignity to the important, yet undervalued work of those who educate the nation's teachers" (37). He agrees with Feldman (2003) and Grossman (2005) who see teacher education research as important political work especially in contexts where there are aggressive and persistent efforts to regulate and control teacher education from the outside (Cochran-Smith, 2006). Like Zeichner, I believe that practitioner-generated knowledge can build the knowledge base in teacher education and professionalisation. In this chapter, I present an auto-ethnographic account of the interaction of my academic and "personal self to the culture" (Ellis & Bochner, 2000:739) of the university.

Auto-ethnography as a qualitative research method gives a unique voice and window into one's lived experiences (Nethsinghe & Southcott, 2015). It offers the researcher the opportunity to interrogate the attitudes, assumptions and beliefs that underpin personal experience, professional practice and educational values (Chang, 2008; De Bruin, 2016). Auto-ethnographers seek to describe, interpret and systematically analyse personal experience to explore cultural (or educational) experiences within social context (Reed-Danahay, 1997). Yet auto-ethnographies of becoming teachers in higher education can also offer wider socially useful insights into how we can "learn, cope and make our way" (Ellis & Adams, 2014:255) as higher education teachers, academics, and researchers. The single study presented here can thus contribute to a wider set of studies in South Africa, including those in this volume, to illustrate and explore higher education teaching in education.

As a self-reflexive research genre in which the multifaceted, contingent self of the researcher becomes a lens through which to study interrelationships between personal autobiographies, lived experiences, and wider social and cultural concerns (Chang, 2008; Ellis & Adams, 2014; Grant, Short & Turner, 2013), this method of research is applicable to the study of my engagements in a PGCE module. The self is a social being who learns to understand others by reflecting about the self in relation to others (Wall, 2006). I want to make visible my professional experience including my feelings and emotions as experienced during the design and teaching of this module. My experience has "resonance beyond the self" (Pithouse, Mitchell & Webb, 2009:43) and can create opportunities for improving practice – my own and that of other academics. Conscious of the fact that "introspection is not an appropriate substitute for data collection" and cannot be used to drive our disciplines forward (Delamont, 2007:1), my aim is not self-obsession but rather to share experiences that have relevance for others in similar situations.

I follow Webster-Wright's (2009) notion of "authentic professional learning, [which encourages] a spirit of critical inquiry where professionals can gain insight into their own learning and the assumptions they hold about their practice" (272). Hayler (2011:3) supports the need to hear the voices of teacher educators through "self-narrative ... lived experience with all its historical, social and cultural contexts ... it follows that experiences of teacher educators offer insights and illumination in this key area of education". Mitchell, Moletsane and De Lange (2015:11) suggest that taking an auto-ethnographic stance to our lives and work as university teachers can enable openness to critical "moments of learning (about ourselves and our students)", with the aim of making a qualitative difference to our teaching and scholarship. Informed by an understanding and appreciation that "cultural realities are perceived differently by people who emerge from the same cultural setting" (Mudaly, 2015:36), I attempt to offer "narrative truth as pragmatic truth" and strives for "verisimilitude and truthfulness" instead of precision and truth (Ashley & Peterson, 2015: 226-227). Like Imsen (1999:95), I believe that "reflection forms an integral part of the very complex enterprise of teaching because it can help us to make sense of the normative expectations and reality". Meloni, Vanthuyne and Rousseau (2015:165) argue that reflective practice, and ultimately reflexivity, is a key means by which teacher educators might be able to equip teachers-to-be with skills and dispositions to question assumptions about teaching and learning in South Africa in the twenty-first century.

The study is based on reflective data obtained from my students' interactions with me, my personal beliefs made explicit in relation to the purpose of education and the role of educators, and my experiences of the institutional expectations of the course and engagements with students, which culminated in reflective field notes (Goodall, 2000). Through reflection on these sources, I try to understand the effect of my engagements with the course and my students on their preparation for the profession. I discuss challenges that include, among others, inheritance of a module with a predominantly functionalist orientation, time constraints (I see students for approximately two hours per week), the general attitudes and expectations of the students as well as perceived disjointedness in the structure of the PGCE course as a whole. Following Vecchio and O'Leary (2004), I use an inductive process to analyse concepts, words or groups of words, non-verbal cues and other elements such as literary devices, and present the data thematically.

The three themes that emerged as challenges for my pedagogy

My reflections centre on the challenges to my pedagogical work so that my students can learn to know their own learners and how they learn. I present these challenges in three themes that emerged as challenges for my pedagogy. Theme one was *working in a regulative environment*. This theme was about balancing adherence to national education policies, the university's graduate attributes and your department's focus on the one hand, whilst having one's own ideas of transformation through a social justice agenda, on the other. At the same time, teaching my students how they should strive for social justice within the confinements of policy, was challenging. The second theme was *knowing who we teach and how they learn*. Teaching a class of 230 students with an array of ethnic, race, class, language and cultural backgrounds posed another challenge for my pedagogy. Students come with a variety of undergraduate disciplinary backgrounds; some are practising professionals, but most are new to teaching. Theme three was *deciding on what knowledge to include in the course.* My struggle revolved around striking a balance between knowledge-for-practice (formal propositional or higher-order knowledge which includes facts, abstract knowledge of ideas and principals) and knowledge-of-practice or practical knowledge. I explain the three themes in more detail below.

Working in a regulative environment

In most countries around the world, there is a plethora of regulations framing teacher education. South Africa is no exception. *Minimum Requirements for Teacher Education Qualifications* (MRTEQ) are formally gazetted in policy outlined by the Department of Higher Education and Training (DHET, 2015) who envisages particular types of educators for South Africa and the world. Such teachers must have particular knowledge, skills and values.

According to the DHET, forms of knowledge for educators include: sound subject knowledge; knowledge of how to teach their subject(s) and how to select, determine the sequence and pace of content in accordance with both subject and learner needs; knowledge of who their learners are and how they learn; understanding of learners' individual needs so that teaching can be tailored accordingly; knowledge of how to communicate effectively, in general, as well as in relation to their subject(s), in order to mediate learning.

The DHET regulations see the prerequisite skills for newly qualified teachers as highly developed literacy, numeracy and information technology (IT) skills; knowledgeability about the school curriculum and its specialised content, as well as being able to use available resources appropriately to plan and design suitable learning programmes. Teachers must also understand diversity in the South African context to ensure they teach in a manner that includes all learners, and can manage classrooms effectively across diverse contexts for a conducive learning environment. They must be able to identify learning or social problems and work in partnership with professional service providers to address these. They need to assess learners in reliable and varied ways, and use the results of assessment to improve teaching and learning.

The values newly qualified teachers need to portray, as per the DHET regulations, include: a positive work ethic and appropriate conduct in a manner that befits, enhances and develops the teaching profession. They should also be able to reflect critically on their own practice in theoretically informed ways and in conjunction with their professional community of colleagues, in order to constantly improve and adapt to evolving circumstances.

Most universities in South Africa (including mine) follow a theory-led inductive approach to teaching with content subjects that focus on general educational theories, subject pedagogies related to the school curriculum and subjects focusing on general pedagogy. My module falls into the category of general pedagogy and incorporates all three spheres (knowledge, skills and values) of the MRTEQ (DHET, 2015) requirements for newly qualified teachers. The outcomes of the module have to be aligned with these national policies. In addition, these outcomes must be aligned with the university's graduate attributes.

My university's graduate attributes of "an enquiring mind, engaged citizen, dynamic professional and well-rounded citizen" (Stellenbosch University, 2012) are framed in education by the conceptual framework of Productive Pedagogies (Hayes, Mills, Christie & Lingard, 2006) that seeks to lead to substantive conversation and identify knowledge as problematic. These formal requirements have to be balanced with the current realities in our school communities.

Ferreira and Schulze (2014:1) suggest that "many schools in South Africa are depicted as sites where disrespect for the law, racial intolerance and violence proliferate". I am mindful of the fact that school violence has reached alarming proportions in South Africa. It is for this very reason that the Department of Basic Education is so committed to the implementation of values via its teachers. The focus on values in education in the curriculum is "firmly grounded on the Constitution of South Africa and the Bill of Rights that provide the rationale for curriculum transformation that mirror the ideals of a democracy" (Ferreira & Schulze, 2014:1).

Bringing these formal requirements together in a programme or single module requires acknowledgement in the curriculum and pedagogy of the identity issues and historical legacies of the country. It is with the graduate attributes and the thinking behind them that I try to open up the lecture room for robust, critical, but respectful discussion. Engaging with constitutional law and values can be a way for the module to open up discussion about what the values mean in practice. Future teachers need help to respond in a productive and creative way to regulative demands and working environments that are constrained by strong aspirations, formal policies and conditions in many poor schools that do not support these aspirations.

In an attempt to help students instill values of democratic citizenship, I lecture and provide readings on teachers' professional and ethical identities in relation to regulative environments of schools, the dominant neoliberal demands of the world of work and how an ethical approach based on social justice can equip learners with tools to assist them to understand themselves and others in more humane ways.

In this section of the module, my students generally show a keen interest as it engages them with clear 'how to do' or 'what to do' methodologies for practice. Students often comment that this section of the work is "very helpful", or "empowering" or "prepares [them] for school". My sense of this kind of feedback is that the current ongoing tensions in schools cause anxiety in students. They need to know what to do to protect themselves or safely navigate the quantitative performative demands and increasingly hostile interactions with learners, their parents and even the education department. Ball's (2003) paper entitled *The teacher's soul and the terrors of performativity* explains the anxiety that confronts both teacher and student in the current education climate. Whilst I have to teach my students how to respond to regulative and hostile environments in school, I must also negotiate the same conditions. A key challenge for novice teachers is to build a sense of agency in relation to requirements, rather than merely compliance. Explicit engagement with the relevant policy requirements and frameworks seems to make it possible to imagine diverse forms of practice for both of us.

Knowing who we teach and how they learn

My students come from different undergraduate disciplinary backgrounds. They have diverse ethnic and cultural backgrounds and for most in the class it is the very first time that they encounter preparations to become teachers. A few students are practising professionals who upskill while others' motivation for a PGCE is diversification of skills to be taken up in the job-market. They therefore have different ways of doing, as well as expectations of – and motivations for – doing the course. Apart from available online platforms, the actual face-to-face teaching engagement time for PGCEs is only about four months in the beginning of the year. During the third term of the teaching year these students undertake their teaching practice in schools. When they return during the fourth term, there is very little time left for teaching, which means that overall there is only a very small window of opportunity available to make an impression on these students in terms of their preparation as teachers.

Apart from knowledge about the general workings of teachers in terms of governance, management and leadership in a classroom and school, I also focus on the aspect of understanding who are the learners we are teaching and how they learn. This competence requires teachers' assessment practices to be based on their knowledge of learning theories, their interpretations of assessment results, their ability to reflect on the results and their own teaching with the aim of improving their teaching and learning practices. Important to remember here is that teaching philosophies, as well as those who do teacher education, have changed radically since 1994. Approaches and practices are now supposed to be based on democratic, inclusive and participative relationships, reflective practice, experimentation and risk-taking. Thus, in my module I focus on the knowledge of different learning theories and their possible impact on educators' teaching strategies and learners' learning in an attempt to enhance teachers' knowledge and understanding of both teacher- and learner-centred approaches, their value and implications for classroom practices.

In their review of curriculum, pedagogy and teaching practices in developing countries, Westbrook et al. (2013) found four theories of learning that underpin different pedagogic approaches: behaviourism, constructivism, social construction and critical pedagogies. In this section I include traditional and non-traditional/unrecognised teaching and learning forms, not only because of my agreement with Schweisfurth (2011) that teaching and learning processes in any classroom are deeply embedded in the cultural, resource, institutional and policy contexts, but also because of my social justice ontological orientations. My logic is also informed by Shields and Mohan's (2008) idea that educators cannot ignore the multiple forms of social, cultural and economic capital their students bring into their schools and must take steps to provide an education that challenges and overcomes inequities. These researchers' emphasis that "consideration of students' lived experiences will enable teachers to understand students' varied socio-economic backgrounds" (in Jwan & Kisaka, 2017:3) speaks to my own orientation to teaching in South Africa, which I carry with me into my classes. By using problem-based methods, I try to entice students into critical writing and discussions on the implications of various classroom and school governance, management and leadership conventions that elicit democratic citizenship values.

The reaction from students in terms of engaging with core and additional literature and participating in classroom discussions is generally low. Students do not read and proverbially 'get under the skin' of concepts such as social justice, democracy, equality, non-racism and non-sexism, ubuntu (human dignity), an open society, accountability, the rule of law, respect and reconciliation. The limited conversations that do take place in class are usually very superficial.

With very few exceptions, the three formal assessment results for the year (online assignments based on core, additional and further readings and the application of key concepts to practice) are generally average. Aspects such as coherence in arguments, substance and criticality are mostly lacking in students' essays. But at the same time, I ask myself: How often do lecturers on the PGCE programme talk among themselves about the overall coherence and alignment in the programme? How often and what kind of academic conversations do we have about our work? What key content would we like to see included? How responsive is our programme to society at large, and what is our collective understanding about democratic citizenship? The silos in which we operate might have prevented us from rigorous academic engagement on the issues we teach.

We implemented the Productive Pedagogy framework with the inception of the new PGCE programme in 2018. In many instances, our module content became reflections of our own particular expressions of content and pedagogy, which set the scene for the following three years. We were keen not to promote a mode of curriculum delivery based on a transmission mode or banking concept, as Freire (1970 in Deans, 1999) describes it. If goals for schooling as a means of building equality and democratic citizenry are to be realised, different pedagogies are needed that allow students to challenge their own identities in relation to 'others' to develop understanding and empathy with people from other groups. Despite our best intentions, our students tell us that we are overlapping and duplicating work. The PGCE programme is jam-packed and my students often complain of not having enough time. There is very little time to get to know them and understand how they learn.

Apart from the official structure of the programme, therefore, it could be that we ourselves still need to work on having a collective understanding of what it is we want to teach in the PGCE course. It could be that we have very different understandings of what education is, of what schools look like and the roles that teachers ought to play. It could be that the lack of shared understanding of the educational project among ourselves is seeping into our lectures and contributes to students feeling unprepared for the realities of school.

What knowledge to include?

Our actions in historic and social contexts give structure to what we do. Therefore, according to Lave and Wenger (1991:50), "there is an interdependent relationality between agent and world, activity, meaning, cognition, learning and knowing". My considerations of the design and delivery of the PGCE module were linked to who I am as a person, my knowledge, experiences and views of education, the particular time in the history of the country and context in which schooling took place in South Africa.

Working with so many different students in my class with diverse racial, cultural, linguistic and political backgrounds, made me feel like working at a border zone. Wenger (1998) and Tuomi-Gröhn and Engeströhm (2003) describe such a zone as an intersection where challenge, contestation and playing out of power relationships happen: a potential site for new learning opportunities and new knowledge. McMillan views teachers as actors who "broker" (2015:229) or facilitate activities across border zones. Teachers as 'boundary workers' are agents who assist participants to make new connections at border zones to open up possibilities for new meaning and learning (Wenger, 1998). My considerations in the PGCE module were informed by the view that the teacher as a border worker can mediate between students' understandings across different border zones.

Two main concepts informed my struggle around what knowledge teachers need. The first is knowledge-for-practice which Cochran-Smith and Lytle (1999) understand to mean formal, propositional or higher-order knowledge that includes facts, abstract knowledge of ideas and principles. The second is knowledge-of-practice or practical knowledge. The discussion is deepened by the debate between proponents of social realist, powerful/vertical knowledge (Bernstein, 1999; Muller, 2009; Shay, 2016; Young, 2005, 2008) and the proponents of horizontal, every day and multiple forms of knowledge (Beck, 2013; Fataar & Feldman, 2016; Feldman & Fataar, 2014; Lyotard, 1984; Wheelahan, 2007; Zipin, 2017; Zipin, Fataar & Brennan 2015) arguing for a more socially just and humane approach to education. A Fraserian social justice orientation (Fraser, 2009) coupled with a Vygotskian (scaffolding) (see Bruner, 1978) approach informs the underlying logic to my teaching.

My thinking around what to include as content knowledge in the module is informed by the debates and tensions around what knowledge is and which knowledge/whose knowledge ought to be prioritised in the curriculum. On the one hand, there is the argument about powerful or disciplinary knowledge, a kind of knowledge that "is produced in specialist knowledge communities"; knowledge that has set "boundaries" of what counts as valid (Young, 2013:108). This kind of knowledge, its proponents claim (Bernstein, 1999, 2000; Muller, 2009, 2014; Shay, 2016), should be prioritised in the curriculum as it offers students the capacity to move beyond their everyday experiences. This vertical/practical/powerful knowledge is argued to be "systematically revisable", "emergent", "real", "material", "social", and produced in "particular socio-epistemic formations" (Muller, 2014:236-238) which can be considered contemporaneously as 'disciplines' (Muller, 2009). This kind of knowledge is seen as important and valued for vocations and work places where students need to negotiate and understand the modern world. Following this line of thinking, education serves to enable students to access (powerful) knowledge that is not available to them in their everyday lives. This kind of knowledge will eventually enable students to move beyond their particular understandings and experience, and help them to gain a better understanding of the world in which they live (Young & Muller, 2007;2013).

The counterargument to this position is that forms of curriculum that are 'aims-based', 'skills based' or 'outcomes based' are problematic in that they are vulnerable to politicisation and instrumentalism (Beck, 2013; Wheelahan, 2007). Beck emphasises the "self-referential" nature of disciplinary discourse as a potential problem for relating powerful knowledge to students' experiences (2013:187). Established, modernist and Euro-centric forms of knowledge are also often more valued than alternative and multiple forms of knowledge (Lyotard, 1984; Zipin et al., 2015). In the South African context specifically, a key problem with abstract, disciplinary knowledge and its power to change and provide opportunities is that it does not always play out in the intended ways. As Feldman and Fataar (2014) note, this can lead to epistemic disaffection for many students in South Africa due to the large disparities of knowledge repertoires and lack of opportunities for induction into powerful knowledge.

Another way of distinguishing different kinds of knowledge is to differentiate between knowledge that is "codified and generalizable" and knowledge that is "event-structured and personal" (Webb, 2007 in Bertram, Mthiyane & Mukeredzi, 2013:449). The first type of knowledge is also described as propositional or higher-order knowledge, which according to these authors includes facts, abstract knowledge of ideas and principles and is mainly about sense making and meaning. This knowledge for practice (Cochran-Smith & Lytle, 1999) is content and pedagogical knowledge. The second type, event-structured and personal knowledge, is described as procedural, practical or context-specific knowledge (Knight, 2002; Wilson & Demetriou, 2007). Stuart, Akyeampong and Croft (2009) and Kennedy (2002) call it 'craft knowledge' that is created in the context of practice. Knowledge of practice helps construct teachers as agents, where teacher knowledge is connected to larger political and social agendas.

My approach to the design and teaching of the Education Governance, Leadership and Management module is to try and strike a balance between normative, vertical knowledge and horizontal, everyday knowledge. In other words, I strive for balance between propositional and context-specific knowledge. I invite my students to read core literature provided in the module, as well as their own additional literature, on how to understand the issues of governance, management and leadership. This is important to address the general workings of teachers in a school, and to understand one's practice as an educator leader, governor or manager in terms of the current realities in the majority of South African schools. I invite class discussions after readings and lectures on the issues and ask for alternative views with evidence. I probe with problem-based case study scenarios, videos, pictures and cartoons in order to elicit critical discussion. Zipin (2017) draws from Fraser (2009) to assert that a problematic-based approach to curriculum holds:

> ... grammar-transforming potentials to advance social educational needs and aspirations of all learners, and especially power marginalised groups that constitute so much of SA's population, through robust cultural inclusion and participatory parity (Fraser, 2009) that, as Fraser suggests, "the times demand." (Zipin, 2017:69)

Such discussions, I feel, provide students with opportunities for robust and yet respectful engagement and co-operative learning. They stimulate further discussion and practice of how to assert themselves in the workplace articulately and with informed voices. However, while there are fruitful class discussions and buy-in from a minority of students, generally the class does not engage in the reading of the core literature, let alone additional literature. My reflection notes on verbal interactions with students read: "long readings are boring"; "too little time"; "just give us the notes"; "nice, but how about more law stuff". In the written reflection sections which form 5% of each of their three assessment activities, students write: "I don't see the relevance of theoretical concepts of governance, management and leadership and what we actually have to do in schools"; "We are under pressure with a lot of assessment, we don't have time to read"; "less theory please!!!"; "Too much time on the moral stuff". Except for a few, most students' essays at the end of the year show only superficial engagement with, and integration of, theory in practice. In my module design, education about education is as important as education for education because you cannot teach what you yourself do not understand. Even after trying a variety of methods to elicit critical discussions in the lecture room, the conversations rarely include three quarters of the class. I am worried that I will succumb to the pressure for decontextualised practical knowledge to the detriment of the ethical knowledge of education.

What I understand from this is that my students might be feeling pressed for time. This could be an indication that the programme is too heavily stacked in terms of the available time. I also sense impatience with the expectation of deep reading and critical discussion and application of knowledge. Again, this could be because of time pressure, or the pressure from schools for practical rather than knowledgeable teachers. Or it may be that the students find such issues too personally confronting.

Donald McIntyre (1995:365) points out that the place of theory in teacher education remains a "source of tension". A common oversimplification is that theory is the domain of the university, and practice is the domain of the school. This view creates an impression among student teachers that university knowledge is "unrealistic" once they operate in the reality of the classroom. It therefore becomes the task of the teacher educator to assist the student teacher in refining (or reframing) their perceptions of teaching and learning.

I have discussed the three themes that emerged as challenges for my pedagogy. I have suggested that future teachers need help to respond in a productive and creative way to regulative demands and working environments that are also constrained by formal policies and conditions in schools. Whilst I had to teach my students how to respond to regulative and hostile environments in school, I had to negotiate the same conditions in the university.

Getting to understand who my students are and how they learnt posed another challenge for my pedagogy. I focused on knowledge of different learning theories and their possible impact on educators' teaching strategies and learners' learning. My teaching in this module attempted to enhance teachers' knowledge and understanding of both teacher- and learner-centred approaches, and their value and implications for classroom practices. Problem-based methods are used to encourage students to write critically and reflect on the implications of educational governance, management and leadership conventions that support democratic citizenship. Unfortunately, students engaged minimally with core and additional literature, and were generally reluctant to participate in classroom discussions. The few conversations that occurred were superficial. Students reported that the programme was very full; that they were under pressure in terms of assessment dates and that there was too little time to engage deeply with readings. Seeing students for only two hours per week also gave me insufficient time to get to know them and how they learnt. The fact that we did not have collective discussions in the PGCE programme about what we teach and whom we teach, could have led to a lack of shared understanding of the educational project, incoherence and misalignment.

Deciding what knowledge to include in the course revolved around debates and tensions about what knowledge is and which knowledge/whose knowledge ought to be prioritised in my module. My approach to the Education Governance, Leadership and Management module was to balance between normative, vertical knowledge and horizontal, everyday knowledge. Fraser's (1995) conceptualisation of social justice informed my consideration of the tension between the redistribution of the policy expectations, recognition of my students' diverse identities and a representation in my lecture content of life world knowledges that students brought with them to the class. While there were fruitful class discussions and buy-in from some students, they were in the minority. Most students did not engage in the reading of the core literature, and certainly not with any additional literature. Students expressed concerns about too little time to read and apathy towards theory and the ethical dimensions of teaching.

Discussion

Education has traditionally been seen as an important socialising arena for preparing students to become active citizens. Higher education is an arena for preparing citizens for democracy and public service. Universities serve as a pipeline in socialising and training prospective teachers to play their part in the establishment of active citizenship in a diverse democracy for the benefit of the community at large. To participate in a democracy, [education] students need to be exposed to a range of competences and multiple perspectives so they can understand and respond to human and social dilemmas in the communities they will teach. Schools, according to Sehr (1997:83):

> ... have long been sites for the 'socialization' of students according to dominant notions of privately oriented democratic citizenship. However, schools can play an important role in promoting alternative understandings of democracy and can thereby help build a more democratic and just society.

Education and socialisation into practice do not happen in a vacuum but is bound up in historical context. Learning is a social practice. It happens for the individual in a social context – a family or a school, for example – and inherits socialised norms or tendencies that guide behaviour and thinking habits and social practices, what Bourdieu calls "habitus" (Bourdieu, 1984:170). When my students walk into the lecture hall, they bring their identities with them. Given the transformative, social justice agenda espoused in the South African constitution and its education policies, teacher educators play a central role in equipping education students with knowledge, skills and values to actualise social justice in society. One of the outcomes deemed desirable by the Higher Education Act (DoE, 1997:2) is that higher education in South Africa should promote the values underlying an open and democratic society based on human dignity, equality and freedom. This is important because of persisting systemic racism and inequality in South African schools and society in general. If the goals for schooling as a means of building equality and democratic citizenry are to be realised, different pedagogies are needed that allow students to challenge their own identities in relation to 'others' to develop understanding and empathy with people from other groups.

In my transformative pedagogy based on social justice principals in the PGCE course, I thought I could help my students relate to difference. To me social justice is the notion that all people in a society deserve fair and equitable rights, opportunities and access to resources. As teacher educators at university, I believe that we do not merely teach subjects, but people; and that education can be a tool for social justice. The purpose of pedagogy for social justice is to interrupt the reproduction of forms of domination (Macrine, McLaren & Hill, 2010) and to question the basis on which equalities are established. Such an approach, I believe, not only applies to marginalised groups (class, 'race', gender, disabilities) that are excluded from full participation, but also provides ways in which the dominant could become part of an ethic of inclusivity. Because knowledge is a social concept, it emphasises the value of multiple perspectives in the teaching/learning experience. It is in this environment that critical questioning can lead to deeper self-reflection as students absorb knowledge and perspectives that differ from their own. I envisaged: "A transformative pedagogy based on social justice principles" that could potentially help students to develop critical consciousness (Castro, 2010:200) about the pervasiveness, sources and implications of structurally embedded inequalities in society. Following Pallisera, Fullana, Palaudàrias and Badosa (2013:587), by combining knowledge of and knowledge about education in this module, I wanted to: "help students discover the profession by preparing them to work in contexts of uncertainty and cope with complex situations".

I had to do a lot of scaffolding between my own identity, the context in which I taught, the regulatory demands of national and university policies, pressures from society to produce ready made uncritical teachers who will fit into the existing discourse of high compliance, as well as my own ideas of what school is for and who and what teachers should be. While knowledge about education is, to me, as important as knowledge for education or practice, my students' increasing lack of engagement with the social justice side of education was worrying. Their often-shallow arguments merely reproduced the content of the study unit in one form or another. I acknowledge that students in a

PGCE course are still developing as independent professional educators, but my concern was the lack of depth, engagement and coherent structure in students' work which can be attributed to the lack of shared understanding of what and for whom schools are for, and what teaching should look like in order to provide society with skills and knowledge to understand themselves in relation to others in more productive ways.

The current performative expectations of teachers and the conditions in which they have to perform their duties in schools also brings about anxiety about inadequate preparation among PGCE students. This brings the type of content and pedagogy in university graduate courses into the spotlight. Apart from the external pressures of schools expecting universities to prepare ready made new teachers for the current regulative environments of schools, lecturers also have to contend with policy expectations about the knowledge, skills and values that teachers need and institutional constraints such as limited time, student and lecturer identities and a possible lack of coherence in the course. This, together with the human dimensions of both students and lecturers, makes finding the right balance between knowledge about education (content knowledge) and knowledge for education (practical knowledge) challenging.

Reflective conversations among colleagues in the course can improve alignment and practice, reduce duplication and increase the healthy balance between knowledge about education and knowledge for education/practice. "Both self and social [reflection], coupled with dialogue can foster a critical consciousness by which students and teachers see their experiences situated in historical, cultural, and social contexts and recognize possibilities for changing oppressive structures" (Nagda, Gurin & Lopez, 2003:168). Reflecting on practice helps one become aware of the importance of reflection for constant improvement, not only on one's practice, but also in terms of personal development.

Conclusion

As part of being socially responsive, universities are engaged in a new paradigm of scholarship where teaching and research is celebrated whilst taking pride in becoming more involved in addressing social problems. A transformative pedagogy based on social justice principals, I argue, can help students relate to difference. Pedagogy for social justice sets out to interrupt the reproduction of forms of domination (Macrine et al., 2010) and to question assumptions underlying establishment of inequalities. This type of approach is not only limited to marginalised groups excluded from full participation, but also provides ways in which dominant groups can become more inclusive.

Reflexivity requires the researcher to take the time to be still, to listen to the internal dialogue and to probe for reactions that are stirred by experience with the data. This journey into the reflections of my engagements in a PGCE module provided me with an opportunity to become not only conscious of how my students engaged with my module, but also how I view myself in relation to my teaching.

References

Ashley, L. & Peterson, R.N. 2015. A case for the use of auto-ethnography in nursing research. *Journal of Advanced Nursing*, 71(1):226-233. https://doi.org/10.1111/jan.12501

Ball, S. 2003. The teacher's soul and the terrors of performativity. *Journal of Education Policy*, 18(2):215-228. https://doi.org/10.1111/jan.12501

Beck, J. 2013. Powerful knowledge, esoteric knowledge, curriculum knowledge. *Cambridge Journal of Education*, 43(2):177-193. https://doi.org/10.1080/0305764X.2013.767880

Berger, P. & Luckmann, T. 1966. *The social construction of reality: A treatise in the sociology of knowledge*. New York: Anchor Books.

Bernstein, B. 1999. Vertical and horizontal discourse: An essay. *British Journal of Sociology of Education*, 20(2):157-173. https://doi.org/10.1080/01425699995380

Bernstein, B. 2000. *Pedagogy, symbolic control and identity*. 2nd Edition. New York, NY: Rowman and Littlefield.

Bertram, C., Mthiyane, N. & Mukeredzi, T. 2013. 'It will make me a real teacher': Learning experiences of part time PGCE students in South Africa. *International Journal of Educational Development*, 33:448-456. https://doi.org/10.1016/j.ijedudev.2012.10.001

Botman, H.R. 2007. A multicultural university with a pedagogy of hope for Africa: Installation speech. Available at: https://bit.ly/38PS67u [accessed 8 June 2020].

Bourdieu, P. 1984. *Distinction: A social critique of the judgement of taste*. London: Routledge.

Bourdieu, P. & Passeron, J.C. 1977. *Reproduction in education, society and culture*. London: Sage.

Bourdieu, P. & Passeron, J.C. 1990. *Theory, culture & society. Reproduction in education, society and culture*. 2nd Edition. (R. Nice, Transl.). London: Sage Publications.

Bruner, J.S. 1978. The role of dialogue in language acquisition. In: A. Sinclair, R. Jarvella & W. Levelt (eds), *The child's conception of language*. Berlin: Springer-Verlag, pp. 241-256.

Castro, A. 2010. Themes in the research on pre-service teachers' views of cultural diversity: Implications for researching millennial pre-service teachers. *Educational Researcher*, 39:198-210. https://doi.org/10.3102/0013189X10363819

Chang, H. 2008. *Autoethnography as method*. Walnut Creek, CA: Left Coast.

Cochran-Smith, M. & Lytle, S. 1999. Relationship of knowledge and practice: Teacher learning in communities. *Review of Research in Education*, 24(1):249-305. https://doi.org/10.3102/0091732X024001249

Cochran-Smith, M. 2006. Policy, Practice, and Politics in Teacher Education. Thousand Oaks, CA: Corwin Press.

Deans, T. 1999. Service-learning in two keys: Paulo Freire's Critical Pedagogy in relation to John Dewey's Pragmatism. *Michigan Journal of Community Service Learning*, 6(1):15-29.

De Bruin, L.R. 2016. The influence of situated and experiential music education in teacher practitioner formation: An autoethnography. *The Qualitative Report*, 21(2):407-427.

Delamont, S. 2007. Arguments against autoethnography. Paper presented at the British Educational Research Association Annual Conference: Institute of Education, University of London, 5–8 September 2007. Available at: https://bit.ly/35H8vcm [accessed 8 June 2020].

DHET (Department of Higher Education and Training). 2015. *Revised policy on the minimum requirements for teacher education qualifications.* Government Gazette No 38487. Pretoria, South Africa: Department of Higher Education and Training.

DoE (Department of Education). 1997. Higher Education Act 101 of 1997. Pretoria: Government Printer. https://doi.org/10.1002/he.9810

Dewey, J. 1933. *How we think. A restatement of the relation of reflective thinking to the educative process.* Revised Edition. Boston: D.C. Heath and Company.

Ellis, C. & Adams, E. 2014. The purposes, practices, and principles of auto-ethnographic research. In: P. Leavy (ed.), *The Oxford handbook of qualitative research.* Oxford: Oxford University Press, pp. 245-276. https://doi.org/10.1093/oxfordhb/9780199811755.013.004

Ellis, C. & Bochner, A. 2000. Autoethnography, personal narrative, reflexivity. In: N. Denzin & Y. Lincoln (eds), *Handbook of qualitative research.* 2nd Edition. Thousand Oaks, CA: Sage, pp. 733-768.

Fataar, A. & Feldman, J. 2016. Dialogical habitus engagement: The twists and turns of teachers' pedagogical learning within a professional learning community. *Perspectives in Education,* 34(3):98-105. https://doi.org/10.18820/2519593X/pie.v34i3.8

Feldman, A. 2003. Validity and quality in self-study. *Educational Researcher,* 32(2):26-28. https://doi.org/10.3102/0013189X032003026

Feldman, J. & Fataar, A. 2014. Conceptualising the setting up of a professional learning community for teachers' pedagogical learning. *South African Journal of Higher Education,* 28(1):1525-1539.

Ferreira, C. & Schulze, S. 2014. Teachers' experience of implementation of values in education in schools: "Mind the gap". *South African Journal of Education,* 34(1):1-11. https://doi.org/10.15700/201412120939

Francis, D. & Le Roux, A. 2011. Teaching of social justice education: the intersection between identity, critical agency, and social justice education. *South African Journal of Education,* 31(3):299-311. https://doi.org/10.15700/saje.v31n3a533

Fraser, N. 1995. From redistribution to recognition? Dilemmas of justice in a "post-socialist" age. *New Left Review,* 1(212): July-August. Available at: https://bit.ly/36GJOvY [accessed 8 June 2020].

Fraser, N. 2009. *Scales of justice: Reimagining political space.* Columbia: Columbia University Press.

Goodall, l. 2000. *Writing the new ethnography.* Boston: Alta Mira Press.

Grant, A., Short, T. & Turner, L. 2013. Introduction: Storying life and lives. In: N. Short, L. Turner & A. Grant (eds), *Contemporary British auto-ethnography.* Rotterdam: Sense, pp. 1-16. https://doi.org/10.1007/978-94-6209-410-9_1

Grossman, P. 2005. Research on pedagogical approaches to teacher education. In: M. Cochran-Smith & K. Zeichner (eds), *Studying teacher education.* San Francisco: Jossey-Bass, pp. 358-389.

Hayes, D., Mills, M., Christie, P. & Lingard, B. 2006. *Teachers and schooling making a difference: Productive pedagogies, assessment and performance.* Crows Nest: Allen & Unwin.

Hayler, M. 2011. *Auto-ethnography, self-narrative and teacher education*. Rotterdam: Sense. https://doi.org/10.1007/978-94-6091-672-4

Howie, S.J., Combrinck, C., Roux, K., Tshele, M., Mtsatse, N., McLeod Palane, N. & Mokoena, G.M. 2017. *ePIRLS 2016: South African Highlights Report*. Pretoria: Centre for Evaluation and Assessment.

Imsen, G. 1999. Reflection as a bridging concept between normative and descriptive approaches to didactics. *Thematic Network on Teacher Education in Europe*, 2(1):95-106.

Jansen, J. 2012. Declare crisis in education. *City Press*, 3 October. Available at: https://bit.ly/2IKTLk4 [accessed 8 June 2020].

Jones, C. 2019. Capital, neoliberalism and educational technology. *Post Digital Science and Education*, 1:288-292. https://doi.org/10.1007/s42438-019-00042-1

Jwan, J. & Kisaka, S. 2017. Democracy, ethics and social justice: Implications for secondary school leadership in Kenya. *South African Journal of Education*, 37(3):1-9. https://doi.org/10.15700/saje.v37n3a1339

Kennedy, M. 2002. Knowledge and teaching. *Teachers and Teaching: Theory and Practice*, 8:355-370. https://doi.org/10.1080/135406002100000495

Knight, P. 2002. A systemic approach to professional development: Learning as practice. *Teaching and Teacher Education*, 18:229-241. https://doi.org/10.1016/S0742-051X(01)00066-X

Kolb, D. 1984. *Experiential learning: Experience as the source of learning and development*. New Jersey: Prentice-Hall.

Lave, J. & Wenger, E. 1991. *Situated learning: Legitimate peripheral participation*. Cambridge: Cambridge University Press. https://doi.org/10.1017/CBO9780511815355

Le Grange, L. 2011. A pedagogy of hope after Paulo Freire. *South African Journal of Higher Education*, 25(1):183-242.

Lingard, B. 2011. Globalising education policy. *Journal of Educational Change*, 12(3):371-377. https://doi.org/10.1007/s10833-011-9170-1

Lyotard, J. 1984. *The postmodern condition: A report on knowledge*. Manchester, NH: Manchester University Press. https://doi.org/10.2307/1772278

Macrine, S., McLaren, P. & Hill, D. (eds). 2010. *Revolutionizing pedagogy. Education for social justice within and beyond global neo-liberalism*. New York: Palgrave MacMillan. https://doi.org/10.1057/9780230104709

Maistry, S. 2014. Education for economic growth: A neoliberal fallacy in South Africa. *Alternation*, 21(1):57-75.

McIntyre, D. 1995. Initial teacher education as practical theorising: A response to Paul Hirst. *British Journal of Educational Studies*, 43(4):365-383. https://doi.org/10.1080/00071005.1995.9974045

McMillan, J. 2015. '[We] have to be ... interpreters to negotiate': Service learning and boundary workers. *South African Journal of Higher Education*, 29(3):222-242. https://doi.org/10.20853/29-3-500

Meloni, F., Vanthuyne, K. & Rousseau, C. 2015. Towards a relational ethics: Rethinking ethics, agency and dependency in research with children and youth. *Anthropological Theory*, 15(1):106-123. https://doi.org/10.1177/1463499614565945

Mezirow, J. 1990. How critical reflection triggers transformative learning. In: J. Mezirow (ed.), *Fostering critical reflection in adulthood*. San Francisco: Jossey-Bass, pp. 1-20.

Mitchell, C., Moletsane, R. & De Lange, N. 2015. Seeing how it works: a visual essay about critical and transformative research in education. *Perspectives in Education*, 33(4):151-176.

Moloi, K. & Henning, E. 2006. A teacher trying to live within and without bias: Making sense in a desegregating place of work. *Education as Change*, 10(2):111-130. https://doi.org/10.1080/16823200609487143

Mudaly, R. 2015. Creating my academic self and space: Autoethnographic reflections on transcending barriers in higher education. *Journal of Education*, 62:35-57.

Muller, J. 2009. Forms of knowledge and curriculum coherence. *Journal of Education and Work*, 22(3):205-226. https://doi.org/10.1080/13639080902957905

Muller, J. 2014. Every picture tells a story: Epistemological access and knowledge. *Education as Change*, 18(2):255-269. https://doi.org/10.1080/16823206.2014.932256

Nagda, B., Gurin, P. & Lopez, E. 2003. Transformative pedagogy for democracy and social justice. *Race Ethnicity and Education*, 6(2):165-191. https://doi.org/10.1080/13613320308199

Nethsinghe, R. & Southcott, J. 2015. A juggling act: Supervisor/Candidate partnership in a Doctoral thesis by publication. *International Journal of Doctoral Studies*, 10, 167185. https://doi.org/10.28945/2256

Pallisera, M., Fullana, J., Palaudàrias, J. & Badosa, M. 2013. Personal and professional development (or use of self) in social educator training. An experience based on reflective learning. *Social Work Education*, 32(5):576-589. https://doi.org/10.1080/02615479.2012.701278

Pithouse, K., Mitchell, C. & Webb, S. 2009. Self-study in teaching and teacher development: a call to action. *Educational Action Research*, 17(1):43-62. https://doi.org/10.1080/09650790802667444

Postma, D. 2016. The ethics of becoming in a pedagogy for social justice. A post humanist perspective. *South African Journal of Higher Education*, 30(3):310-328. https://doi.org/10.20853/30-3-651

Prah, K. 2002. Race and culture: Myth and reality. In: N. Duncan, P. Gqola, M. Hofmeyer, T. Shefer, F. Malunga & M. Mashige (eds), *Discourses on difference, discourses on oppression*. Cape Town: Centre for Advanced Studies of African Society (CASAS) Book Series, pp. 24:9-36.

Reed-Danahay, D. 1997. Leaving home: Schooling stories and the ethnography of autoethnography in rural France. In: D. Reed-Danahay (ed.), *Auto-ethnography: Rewriting the self and the social*. Oxford: Berg, pp. 123-144.

Schoeman, T. 2018. The spatial influence of Apartheid on the South African city. *The Geography Teacher*, 15(1):29-32. https://doi.org/10.1080/19338341.2017.1413002

Schön, D. 1987. *Educating the reflective practitioner*. San Francisco: Jossey-Bass.

Schweisfurth, M. 2011. Learner-centred education in developing country contexts: From solution to problem? *International Journal of Educational Development*, 31(5):425-432. https://doi.org/10.1016/j.ijedudev.2011.03.005

Sehr, D. 1997. *Education for public democracy*. Albany, NY: Suny Press.

Shay, S. 2016. Curricula at the boundaries. *Higher Education*, 71(1):767-779. https://doi.org/10.1007/s10734-015-9917-3

Shields, C. & Mohan, E. 2008. High-quality education for all students: putting social justice at its heart. *Teacher Development*, 12(4):289-300. https://doi.org/10.1080/13664530802579843

Singh, M. 1997. Identity in the making. *South African Journal of Philosophy*, 16(3):120-123.

Spaull, N. 2013. It's the teacher's lack of subject knowledge, stupid. *Sunday Times*, 18 August: p. 6.

Spaull, N. 2018. *South Africa's education crisis: The quality of education in South Africa 1994–2011* (Report commissioned by CDE). Johannesburg, South Africa: Centre for Development and Enterprise (CDE).

Stellenbosch University. 2012. *Graduate attributes*. Available at: https://bit.ly/36PhrM2 [accessed 8 June 2020].

Strom, K.J. & Martin, A.D. 2013. Putting philosophy to work in the classroom: Using rhizomatics to deterritorialize neoliberal thought and practice. *Studying Teacher Education*, 9(3):219-235. https://doi.org/10.1080/17425964.2013.830970

Stuart, J., Akyeampong, K. & Croft, A. 2009. *Key issues in teacher education. A source book for teacher educators*. Oxford: McMillan.

Tuomi-Gröhn, T. & Engeström, Y. (eds). 2003. *Between school and work: New perspectives on transfer and boundary crossing*. Amsterdam: Pergamon.

Vecchio, T. & O'Leary, K. 2004. Effectiveness of anger treatments for specific anger problems: A meta-analytic review. *Clinical Psychology Review*, 24(1):15-34. https://doi.org/10.1016/j.cpr.2003.09.006

Vygotsky, L.S. 1978. *Mind in society: The development of higher psychological processes*. In: M. Cole, V. John-Steiner, S. Scribner & E. Souberman (eds), Cambridge, MA: Harvard University Press.

Wall, S. 2006. An autoethnography on learning about autoethnography. *International Journal of Qualitative Methods*, 5(2):146-160. https://doi.org/10.1177/160940690600500205

Webster-Wright, A. 2009. Reframing professional development through understanding authentic professional learning. *Review of Educational Research*, 79(2):702-739. https://doi.org/10.3102/0034654308330970

Wenger, E. 1998. *Communities of practice: Learning, meaning and identity*. Cambridge: Cambridge University Press. https://doi.org/10.1017/CBO9780511803932

Westbrook, J., Durrani, N., Brown, R., Orr, D., Pryor, J., Boddy, J. & Salvi, F. 2013. Pedagogy, curriculum, teaching practices and teacher education in developing countries. Final Report: Education Rigorous Literature Review. Department for International Development, UK.

Wheelahan, L. 2007. How competency-based training locks the working class out of powerful knowledge: A modified Bernsteinian analysis. *British Journal of Sociology of Education*, 28(5):637-651. https://doi.org/10.1080/01425690701505540

Wilson, E. & Demetriou, H. 2007. New teacher learning: substantive knowledge and contextual factors. *The Curriculum Journal*, 18:213-229. https://doi.org/10.1080/09585170701589710

World Economic Forum, 2016. Future of jobs: Employment, skills and workforce strategy for the Fourth Industrial Revolution. Available at: https://bit.ly/3fbNJEJ [accessed 8 June 2020].

Young, M. 2005. The knowledge question and the future of education in South Africa: A reply to Michelson's 'On trust, desire and the sacred: A response to Johan Muller's Reclaiming Knowledge'. *Journal of Education*, 32:7-17.

Young, M. 2008. From constructivism to realism in the sociology of the curriculum. *Review of Research in Education*, 32:1-28. https://doi.org/10.3102/0091732X07308969

Young, M. 2013. Overcoming the crisis in curriculum theory: A knowledge-based approach. *Journal of Curriculum Studies*, 45(2):101-118. https://doi.org/10.1080/00220272.2013.764505

Young, M. & Muller, J. 2007. Truth and truthfulness in the sociology of educational knowledge. *Theory & Research in Education*, 5(2):173-201. https://doi.org/10.1177/1477878507077732

Young, M. & Muller, J. 2013. On the powers of powerful knowledge. *Review of Education*, 1(3): 229-250. https://doi.org/10.1002/rev3.3017

Zeichner, K. 2007. Accumulating knowledge across self-studies in teacher education. *Journal of Teacher Education*, 58(1):36-46. https://doi.org/10.1177/0022487106296219

Zeichner, K. & Liston, D. 2014. *Reflective teaching: An introduction.* 2nd Edition. New York: Routledge. https://doi.org/10.4324/9780203771136

Zipin, L., Fataar, A. & Brennan, A. 2015. Can social realism do social justice? Debating the warrants for curriculum knowledge selection. *Education as Change*, 19(2):9-36.

Zipin, L. 2017. Pursuing a problematic-based curriculum approach for the sake of social justice. *Journal of Education*, 69:67-92. https://doi.org/10.1080/16823206.2015.1085610

6

Teacherly being and becoming on the PGCE programme: The early emergence of students' reflexive mediations of curriculum knowledge and pedagogy on the History and Sociology of Education module

Aslam Fataar & Jennifer Feldman

Introduction

Situated in the context of teaching in higher education, this chapter provides a discussion on how student teachers on a Postgraduate Certificate in Education (PGCE) module mediate their 'teacherly becoming' (Fataar, 2012) as pre-service teachers. The chapter presents the argument that learning to become a professional teacher involves not only what the students are learning, but also who they are and who they are becoming. Fataar (2012) describes the intersection between how students learn and their acquisition of pedagogical subject content knowledge, as they move through a teacher education programme, as their 'teacherly becoming'. This process, Fataar argues, involves pre-service teachers navigating across:

> the complex performative space of higher education ... the challenging environments of schools in which they do their teaching practice ... and the space of their lives, rooted in their biographies, which they transact across complex urban and rural spaces. (2012:38)

Thus, learning to become a professional teacher involves not only what the student is learning, but also *who* they are becoming. It involves an "integration of knowing, acting, and being in the form of professional ways of being that unfold over time" (Dall'Alba, 2009).

The question posed in this chapter is: How did the content, pedagogy and assessment of a PGCE module titled 'History and Sociology of Education', and sub-titled 'Diversity and Inclusivity', impact on students' 'becoming' as pre-service teachers? We unpack this question by discussing how the knowledge structure or content of this module is connected with, and contributed to, their 'being and becoming' in their PGCE year as pre-service teachers.

Data for the chapter are drawn from student assignments, what we call 'self-writings', which invited students to draw on the module readings and class discussions to consider their positioning as intentional/unintentional bearers of the past. The assignment required them to consider how their emerging reflexivities as student teachers are influenced by their personal and educational backgrounds; and how these reflexivities affected their 'becoming' as student teachers on the PGCE (PGCE assignment 2017). This question required the students to draw on module readings and class and tutorial discussions to consider how their life trajectories had positioned them in their 'becoming' as student teachers during the PGCE module. They were asked to consider this positioning in relation to the content and knowledge structure of the module's focus. Data are presented and discussed according to four themes that emerged from the student essays. The chapter concludes by suggesting that modules that prepare student teachers for the complexity of the teaching profession and interaction with their students will be more productive if opportunities are provided, in the module's assessment modalities, for the students to reflexively engage with aspects of their 'being and becoming' as pre-service teachers.

The module exposes students to readings and discussion on the complex and multiple dynamics that inform racial, class, cultural, linguistic, gender and other patterns of difference and diversity in schools. The focus of the module is on providing students with a conceptual platform for understanding how diversity and inclusion could be engaged with and mediated in educational environments based on a framing of social justice. The module uses Fraser's (1997) notion of social justice to invite students to consider the tension between the redistribution of school knowledge, as for example is currently encoded in the *South African Curriculum and Assessment Policy Statement* (CAPS) (DBE, 2014), on the one hand, and on the other hand the need to recognise and work with the life-world knowledges and social-identity formations of the students. To develop students' conceptualisation of a social justice framing of education, the module includes readings that discuss the dynamics of students' social relations in schools, the formation of student learning identities via their social positioning in schools and a consideration of how student subjectivities are established in their search for quality schooling. The module concludes by providing students with an introduction to a conceptualisation of a more pedagogically just teaching orientation. They are invited to consider alternatives as to how they, as socially just educators, can engage all their learners in the school setting.

Given this specific focus and framing of the module, this chapter discusses how PGCE students within the History and Sociology of Education class were beginning to critically reflect on their 'doxic' (Bourdieu, 1977) assumptions. These assumptions are based on socialisation as seen through their personal life histories and experiences growing up in a particular family and community, which positions them in particular ways as pre-service teachers. Doxic assumptions refer to a set of core values and discourses within a social field that are viewed as inherently true and necessary. Bourdieu refers to them as 'doxa', or what is colloquially taken as the prevailing common discourses about education among pre-service teachers. For Bourdieu, however, doxa, or the 'doxic attitude' means "bodily submission, unconscious submission" (Bourdieu & Eagleton, 1992:121) to conditions that are in fact quite arbitrary and contingent on the social discourses of which they are part, an aspect on which we elaborate further in the chapter.

The essays were based on an invitation to the students to present their analyses of how the module content and class discussions provided them with an engaging and challenging platform that allowed them to consider alternative responses to educational conundrums associated with school going. These alternative responses might be different to those usually informed by their relations within their homes, communities and other educational contexts. Many of the PGCE students, by their own admission in their essay self-writings, grew up in families and communities, within social and cultural environments that are similar to the schools and tertiary institutions they have attended. In other words, they exemplified a large degree of cultural correspondence. What this means is that many of the students have developed a form of subjective knowledge about society, education and student learning based on the way the knowledge, ideas and objects were structured within the relatively narrow confines of the social and cultural fields they moved through. Their form of knowledge is subjectively influenced by their personal, intuitive and social connections and relations in their life worlds, and thus the way in which they come to view the world. What the PGCE module aimed to do, therefore, was to challenge or interrupt the students' subjective ways of knowing, in other words their doxa, by providing readings, lectures and tutorial discussions that enabled them to begin to reflexively interact with their own doxic assumptions that had formed over time.

This chapter starts by situating the discussion within the post-apartheid higher education landscape. Included in this section is an outline of the PGCE module 'History and Sociology of Education: Diversity and Inclusivity' that we presented at our previously white Afrikaans university in the Western Cape. We describe the conceptual and theoretical underpinnings of the module, as this provides an understanding of the knowledge content that informed the students' reflexive responses to the assignment question posed. An understanding of who the students are within the university context is important in the analysis of their self-writings, and we therefore provide an overview of the students within the PGCE cohort. Following this, a discussion of the methodology used to analyse student essays is presented, before moving to a presentation and discussion of aspects of the students' self-writings. In this section we provide analytical themes of the student essays and a discussion on how the students begin to reflexively interact with the intellectual content in the module though class and tutorial discussions, and how these were beginning to impact on their self-formations and 'teacherly becoming' (Fataar, 2012) as pre-service teachers. The chapter concludes by suggesting that modules that prepare student teachers for the complexity of the teaching profession and interaction with their students will be more productive if opportunities in the module's assessment modalities are included which enable them to reflexively engage with aspects of their 'being and becoming' as pre-service teachers.

Knowledge and 'becoming' of university students in post-apartheid South Africa

In 1994 South Africa ushered in a new democracy based on values of inclusivity and equity, which have imbued much of the country's formal policymaking. The South African democratic government committed itself to an array of transformation-oriented initiatives in the higher education sector that sought to effect institutional change in line with the new constitution.

Most of the PGCE students today have not experienced the deep racial divisions associated with the apartheid era, and as a result are less inclined to check their thinking and attitudes about race and discrimination and their impact on ongoing forms of exclusion. Many of the students define themselves as part of the new democratic South Africa without critical interrogation as to how they, or their family members, are positioned within the post-apartheid South African landscape. What is often ignored is the way in which aspects of the past – aspects which are often unconsciously formed, or as Jansen (2010) describes it, "knowledge in the blood" – have positioned students within their families and communities. Jansen refers here to the views, beliefs, values and attitudes which young South Africans have acquired from their homes and community contexts through indirect or "inherited knowledge" (Jansen, 2010:60). Jansen argues that university students who were born after 1994, despite being raised and educated in South Africa's new democracy, have inherited a form of indirect knowledge from their homes and communities. It is this knowledge which unconsciously informs students' knowledge of themselves and others as an embedded dominant belief system that gives meaning, emotion and authority (Jansen, 2010:60) to how the students think, behave and act.

Jansen's notion of indirect or inherited knowledge can be found as operative in Bourdieu's concepts of doxa, habitus and field. Bourdieu describes doxa as a form of discourse and practice of certain beliefs and assumptions that circulate powerfully in everyday settings. Doxa constitute an underlying logic that seems more-or-less unquestionable; while habitus refers to a "system of cognitive and motivating structures" or dispositions that function as "principles that generate and organise practices" (Bourdieu, 1990:53) that have been formed over time. According to Bourdieu, a 'field of play' can be understood as a structured social space or force field within which interactions, transactions and events occur at a specific time and location (Thomson, 2008). A field is not a static entity but fluid and dynamic, and particular practices within a field should not only be seen as a product of habitus, but rather as: "the product of the *relation between* the habitus, on the one hand, and the specific contexts or 'fields' within which individuals act, on the other" (Thompson, 1991:14; italics in original). Relating doxa to habitus and field, Bourdieu writes: "Doxa is the relationship of immediate adherence that is established in practice between a habitus and the field to which it is attuned, the pre-verbal taking-for-granted of the world that flows from practical sense" (1990:68). In other words, doxa can be considered as an individual's sense of reality that "causes practices" or makes one's practices seem sensible, or even a social necessity (1990:68).

What this means for the PGCE students is that over time they have become positioned within the logic of particular societal structural formations that have acquired a taken-for-grantedness that is perceived as 'natural' for all. Concomitantly, these 'positionings' have produced in the students' habitus a form of doxa, a set of beliefs or practices that have become incorporated into their thinking at an almost pre-conscious level. Unless brought to consciousness and interrogated, these beliefs and practices will continue to inform their 'way of being' going forward. Bourdieu states that the habitus is able to be transformed (or added to) by social action and experiences, and continues "from restructuring to restructuring" (Bourdieu, 1977:87) or, as Wacquant (2014:7) suggests, the layering of one's habitus takes place as "any system of transposable schemata that becomes grafted subsequently [onto the habitus], through specialized pedagogical labor".

Developing this, we refer to the students' 'learning habitus' as a layer of habitus formation which over time becomes grafted on to their existing early-formed habitus. One's habitus is not a pre-programmed, automated response to situations, but rather an internalised unconscious relationship between one's embodied dispositions and a social field (Maton, 2008:51). Thus, Bourdieu proposes that to critically analyse the basis on which one's habitus has been formed requires an attitude of ongoing reflexivity where we: "step back and gain distance from dispositions" (Bourdieu & Wacquant, 1992:136). What Bourdieu is suggesting is that transformative action by an individual requires a reflexive response that takes into account how one's social and cultural backgrounds, positioned within particular fields and imbued with intellectual and cultural bias, have shaped the way one views the social world. For Bourdieu, reflexivity requires individuals to engage with a "systematic exploration of the unthought categories of thought which delimit the thinkable and predetermine the thought" (Bourdieu & Wacquant, 1992:40). We suggest this transformation as a form of habitus 'layering' occurs as students begin to reflexively engage with their 'teacherly becoming' in relation to the module content. Our module attempts to engender a reflexive capacity among the students about the ways their doxa is lodged in their habitus and how it can be shifted over time.

Considering how the PGCE students began the process of reflexivity, we propose that this takes place as an interplay between the students' 'learning habitus' (that is the layering of new knowledge through the readings and class discussions) and their doxa, that is their 'taken-for-granted' assumptions that hitherto informed their thinking and practice. The interplay started to enable a process that we describe as a 'pedagogy of discomfort'. By this we refer to the unsettling of the students' 'ways of knowing' that had been unconsciously (or without reflection) formed over time given the social spaces they have inhabited.

We argue that disruption of the doxic assumptions that have formed the pre-service teachers' views of students and schooling in society, requires a deep and reflexive engagement with their own 'ambiguities of becoming' (see Dall'Alba, 2009). As stated by Thomson (2004), who draws on Heidegger:

> ... the very way reality shows up for us is filtered through and circumscribed by the stand we take on ourselves, the embodied life-projects which organize our practical activities and so shape the intelligibility of our worlds. (444)

Thus, the PGCE student cohort were invited to consider their subjective positionings, via a reflexive consideration of issues of diversity and inclusivity as presented in the knowledge component of the PGCE module. While certain themes were outlined and discussed within the class, very little further direction was provided for the students who chose this assignment. It was hoped that the students would take up the themes from the module that were pertinent to their personal biographies and life-world contexts and experiences, and discuss those which had impacted on their 'becoming', their unfolding educational identities as pre-service teachers.

Engaging the PGCE student cohort

The PGCE student group is a large (190 students) and relatively diverse group in terms of their undergraduate studies, and aspects such as race, class, culture, age, language and gender. Three quarters of the students enrolled are female (approximately 150 students out of 190) while the racial component of the class is 118 white, 66 coloured, 3 Indian and 3 black African students. The class represents a fairly even split between English and Afrikaans with 104 students stating that English is their home language and 86 naming Afrikaans as their first language. On the university forms completed for administration purposes, no students give any other language as their home language.

Students enrolling for the PGCE programme are required to have two teaching subjects from their undergraduate degrees for them to be accepted into the one-year post-graduate programme that prepares them to become high school teachers in their specialist subject area. The students enter the PGCE from a variety of disciplines, such as Bachelor of Commerce, Science, Arts, Sport Science, Music, Drama and Art. Some students have also had work experience either in education (such as teaching English in Korea) or in other work sectors, or have completed their Honours or Masters degrees before deciding to complete their PGCE to qualify as a teacher. The mix of students in the class invites the potential for engaging and interactive class discussions from a variety of different perspectives.

Due to the size of the class and limited time allocated (the module offers two fifty minute classes per week), students are provided with all the module readings beforehand and asked to read and engage with specific texts before arriving in class. PowerPoint slides are placed on the university's digital platform for students to access before the lectures. The slides guide them through the class texts and assist them with their reading of the module texts. At times the classes consist of a more lecture-style explanation of theory or concepts; however, despite the large class format, students are invited to draw on their previous knowledge and experience to engage in discussion and debate on the educational topics presented in the lectures. The focus of the classes is to challenge the students, via intellectual content, questions and class debate, to develop a set of reflexive responses to the educational problems discussed. Classes are structured intentionally around a type of learning that teachers in schools can engage their learners in; one that invites the learners into in-depth and challenging discussions. Thus, the module sets out to model a pedagogical approach which the pre-service teachers could consider emulating as a means of meaningfully engaging school children in the curriculum content.

Included in the structure of the module are smaller tutorial groups that students can choose to attend. These groups are intended to provide students with the opportunity to ask questions, discuss, debate and challenge aspects of the module and readings in a smaller group setting. It is often in these groups that students begin to insert themselves and their own biographies into the intellectual dimensions of the module due to the intimacy of the type of discussion that can be facilitated in a smaller group setting. The tutorials tend to provide a safe and more personal environment where students are more inclined to share some of their life experiences and make connections between their personal life-worlds and the theoretical, ethical and conceptual issues presented in the module readings. These are productive sessions and it has been our experience that the students who make the time to attend and engage in the tutorial groups are more able to reflexively grapple with their personal histories and positions in relation to aspects of the intellectual content of the module.

The self-writing assessment option

The module has three assessment opportunities: a class test in the first quarter, an assignment in the second quarter and an exam at the end of the year. It was the mid-year assignment where students were given the option of writing a reflective essay that forms the empirical basis of this chapter. The methodology employed for the study involves a discursive analysis of students' essays as a form of student 'voice'. The essay assignment invited the students to respond to a question that involved a reflexive engagement between their life histories and experiences within the homes and communities they grew up, and the intellectual content of the module that is situated in the complex dynamics of diversity and inclusivity within the South African context. This required the students to work with the theoretical and conceptual frameworks and module readings that we provided and draw from the class and tutorial discussions to critically reflect on their positioning as pre-service teachers. The reflective essay was framed as follows:

> "It is not the consciousness of man that determines their being, but, on the contrary, their social being that determines their consciousness" (Tucker, 1978:4 in Panofsky, 2003:2). With reference to this quotation and drawing on the readings and discussions in the PGCE History and Sociology of Education module, write a reflective essay that discusses the educational dilemmas that you experience as a pre-service teacher. You should specifically discuss your positioning as an intentional/unintentional bearer of the past as a core part of your 'becoming' as a pre-service teacher.

Twenty-six students chose to write the reflective essay. In the next section, we discuss these essays as a way of understanding how, or in what way, the intellectual content of the History and Sociology of Education module intersects with the students' 'becoming' as pre-service teachers.

Student self-writings: Analysis and discussion

The twenty-six student essays offer a diverse and rich description of the students' background positioning and personal experiences in terms of which they had developed their personal and educational assumptions over time. They further provide insight into how, as PGCE students, they were engaging with the module content via readings, class discussion and tutorial groups, and how this module's reflexive processes were able to facilitate shifts in their thinking about their professional role as an educator.

The students who form the focus of this analysis are diverse in terms of race, class, culture, language and gender. One student (all names are pseudonyms), reflecting on aspects of diversity in her essay, states:

> One cannot argue that colonisation together with the apartheid government has not left people wounded directly or indirectly. It has left a bitter taste that affects us all whether we pretend not to see it or act towards it. It made us see race, colour, culture and religion before seeing the human being in front of us ... if we do not acknowledge diversity in our schools then we will be teaching our students that they are all the same when in fact we are all different because of who we are, where we come from and what we bring with us to our education. These differences are supposed to be embraced, cherished and recognised. (Emily)

The students presented aspects of their biographies in their essays and describe how their life experiences constructed their educational assumptions, what we refer to as their doxa of education. Their set of beliefs or practices that have formed a taken-for-granted logic or reality over time, has informed their thinking about education and educational practices.

Four groups of pre-service teachers emerged in the self-writing essay responses linking their student biographies and how these informed their personal and pedagogical identifications during the module. The first group includes two black African students who completed their undergraduate degrees at a different university, arriving at Stellenbosch for the first time at the start of their PGCE year; the second group comprised three homosexual white males; the third group consisted of three coloured students, and the fourth and largest group was made up of sixteen white students. What follows is a discussion of how each group was positioned and how its members' learning habitus encountered the module's emphasis on the need for students to reflexively engage in their 'teacherly becoming' in diverse educational circumstances.

Wounds from the past: "A bitter taste that affects us all"

Bongiwe, one of the students from the first group, describes herself as a black African from a rural background. She completed her undergraduate studies at a university close to the rural community where she lived as a child. Watching her mother as a factory worker walk long distances in adverse weather conditions made her vow to "make something out of my life, daily wanting so badly to study hard and change my family situation". Bongiwe notes that she attended the village school but always hoped that one day she could attend a former Model C school where she could learn to speak, read and write English. The opportunity came during her high school years, but this required that she move from her village and live with her aunt in an urban setting very different to where she had grown up. Her desire for a quality education was greater than the challenges of adapting to the new lifestyle which she describes as follows:

> ... everything was different from the busy streets to the boys by the corner taverns who always made me uncomfortable ... but I had to find a way to fit in without compromising myself, my desire to attend the school was great. (Bongiwe)

Bongiwe completed her high school education and obtained marks that allowed her to follow her dream of studying at a university. She completed her undergraduate studies at the University of Fort Hare, obtaining a Bachelor of Science degree in Chemistry. However, once she had completed her studies, she struggled to find a job as she had no computer or access to the internet or transport to go into the city to search for a job. Six months after graduating from university one of the local village high schools where she lived offered her a school governing body post, teaching Mathematics. This position opened the door for her to apply for other teaching positions and the following year she was offered a permanent position at a private school in the nearby city area. She describes the experience as extremely difficult, stating that she:

> ... struggled, not with the content delivery, but to understand how the school operates, so many things were foreign to me and I had to find a way to fit in ... thanks to today's technology I was able to download movies that were based on private schooling experiences which helped me understand what I needed to do. (Bongiwe)

Bongiwe says that this is how she "fell in love with teaching and ... decided to apply to Stellenbosch University to study to become a qualified teacher". She describes the dissonance that she felt between her background and Stellenbosch University on her arrival at the university:

> Everything about Stellenbosch University was different – the culture and the language – to a point where I felt that I was too black to be there. I lived in constant panic and fear of not being able to pass. Yes, I was a university graduate but the University of Fort Hare was different. I could relate to the students there; I made friends, spoke my mother tongue to my classmates ... here it was different and some students didn't want to speak English ... people kept asking: "What made you decide to come and study here?" I felt like people saw me as a person who did not belong here. (Bongiwe)

Bongiwe's positioning in her PGCE year highlights the vulnerability of students navigating an unfamiliar, culturally dissonant university environment. She chose to attend Stellenbosch University as she perceived it as being able to provide her with a quality postgraduate education that would enable her to teach in schools that she was unable to access as a child.

In Bongiwe's assignment narrative she describes how she was unprepared for the level of 'difference' that she viscerally felt when having to deliver a lesson in English to a group of students who come to Stellenbosch University as part of the micro-teaching educational programme. Each week different PGCE students are allocated lessons to present to a group of school learners who are brought to the university from local schools. Bongiwe was assigned to give students from an 'elite' school an English lesson. She felt that the students responded differently to her than to her white peers, especially as the learners often asked her to repeat what she said as they were unable to understand her accent. Already feeling like an "outsider to Stellenbosch University", she describes this experience as "one of her nightmares".

A second student, Sandisile, also came to Stellenbosch University for the first time as a post-graduate student. Resonant with Bongiwe's experiences, he states:

> I attended a disadvantaged school that did not prepare me for what was expected in my PGCE year, especially when delivering a lesson to learners from a private school who, even though I delivered the lesson in English, ... still kept raising their hands telling me they did not understand what I was saying. (Sandisile)

Bongiwe reflects on her experiences by drawing on the History and Sociology of Education module readings. She describes how the experiences of learners accessing quality schooling in post-apartheid South Africa (see Fataar, 2015) resonated with her own experiences and determination to move beyond how she feels her life had originally positioned her: as a rural, mostly non-English speaking person, destined to follow in the foot-steps of her factory-worker mother. For her, being an unintentional bearer of the past meant that she keenly felt her positioning as a black African from a rural village as a pre-service teacher within the context of Stellenbosch University. In turn, Sandisile wrote that for him the differences in cultural ways of being was the aspect that impacted most on him. He stated that, "Students here are different and thus respect for teachers varies. Some students react differently when they are faced with a pre-service teacher". He describes his experience of teaching some school student groups as undermining his confidence during his time at Stellenbosch.

The process of reflection for both students enabled them to consider how to shift their current perceptions of themselves in relation to their experiences during their PGCE year. Bongiwe states:

> We cannot run away from our past and how it has positioned us, but I feel that all the bloodshed, the tears, the hatred that has been going on for years in this country will stay in our veins if we as new teachers do not go out there knowing ourselves or if we hide behind the facts by saying that we do not see colour. (Bongiwe)

Thus for Bongiwe and Sandisile, engagement with the History and Sociology of Education module's concepts and discussions had to turn to finding ways to navigate a different way forward in their 'teacherly becoming', a way of moving into the future.

"Hiding in plain sight": Fitting in with the dominant rhetoric of social spaces

All three of the second group of students identify as gay men. The first student, Calvin, describes himself as a white, Afrikaans, cisgender, homosexual male. He describes his schooling as taking place in a public middle-class school, a "homophobic space". In contrast, when completing his undergraduate studies in a small music department, Calvin states that his identity as a gay male was considered the 'norm' as heterosexual men in this department were rare and even "frowned upon". The open acceptance of his identity as a gay male during his tertiary studies has, according to Calvin, allowed him to drop the façade of heteronormativity and embrace his "queer male identity". What he fears now, as he reflects on his 'teacherly becoming' as an educator in the South African school context is "entering a world where my identity and even more so, my views, would be inhibited".

In Calvin's essay he engages with the conceptual and theoretical aspects of the module readings to discuss his 'educational becoming' as a gay male within what he describes as a dominant culture or 'norm' of heteronormativity that he feels currently exists within South African schools. Using Bourdieu, one of the theorists discussed in the module, Calvin describes heteronormativity as a 'doxic attitude' that is manifested "through the symbolic representations that are present in school systems where some are advantaged while others are disadvantaged due to the possession or lack of capital ... or appropriate actions ... in accordance with the rules in the field" (Calvin). Citing Samuel (2013:403), Calvin goes on to state that: "Queer or LGBT people experience injustices as their gender and sexuality is excluded and embodies a 'devalued cultural capital'".

Within the History and Sociology of Education module, aspects of inclusion and exclusion in relation to learners accessing different school contexts is discussed. Calvin refers to this discussion and relates it to his own feelings of inclusion and exclusion stating:

> Regardless of the legitimacy of the agents who do not have the symbolic capital (victims of symbolic violence), due to the relations in the field, their arguments will not be recognised ... or may be marginalised in a space in order to create a normative

> behaviour for the space. This would refer to non-heterosexual portrayals in a heteronormative space ... which can easily be seen in the way LGBT or queer bodies are silenced in schools where they are being bullied. (Calvin)

Considering how this impacts on his 'teacherly becoming' as a pre-service teacher, Calvin notes:
> In a heteronormative school environment I do not have the 'gender capital'. My mannerisms, interests, talents and language usage do not speak of masculinity at all. This could therefore negatively influence my relational positioning in the school. Teachers and learners who have the normative habitus would be able to be positioned above me ... I am conscious of the fact that I would not enjoy the same privileges as my heterosexual counterparts ... such as being able to make reference to my sexuality, my partner or life events as easily and freely as heterosexual teachers could easily do. (Calvin)

Calvin has come to understand how Bourdieu's notion of cultural (symbolic) capital highlights how individuals are able to advance their endeavours when they perform contextually or socially correct behaviour, noting that: "this would be where heteronormativity or masculinity or the binary view of gender and sexuality is awarded". Thus, in social structures such as schools, non-heteronormative individuals may experience conflict and could be excluded or marginalised.

Calvin, along with the other two PGCE students who identify as cisgender and homosexual, drew on Bourdieu's concept of habitus not only to understand how their own teaching and identity may be influenced when teaching in a heteronormative schooling system, but also how this has assisted them to understand how other forms of marginalisation position learners in schools.

Referring to the module readings and class and tutorial discussions, Alan (another student who identifies as gay) notes:
> Coming from a relatively conservative white farming background my habitus is comprised of certain aspects — such as respect for one's elders and being courteous ... but also includes aspects which involve treating people differently based on visible and invisible aspects of their identity (race, religion, sexual orientation). (Alan)

Reflecting on this, he goes on to state that he has come to realise that teachers easily
> ... fall into a set of beliefs that are considered normal; what Bourdieu refers to as doxa that leads to the misrecognition of the forms of cultural capital that learners possess and that can be harnessed in order to aid academic achievement. (Alan)

The essays of the three students who identify as gay reveal a substantial level of reflexive engagement through their interaction with the module content and class and tutorial discussions. They draw on their own experiences of being marginalised in schools. Calvin notes that due to his experience as a gay male in the schooling system where "LGBT or queer bodies were silenced ... and bullied", he has begun to challenge his own thinking on how he can find ways to ensure that he does not perpetuate forms of symbolic violence in his own teaching. Alan, similarly notes:

> ... I have come to the conclusion that teaching is about vulnerability. Moreover, effective teaching is about being confident in one's vulnerability in order to relate to, and possibly inspire, learners by showing that we are as human as they are and that our academic prowess is something attainable, instead of coming across as mighty glass towers alienating learners from the education process or intimidating them by coming across as (superficially) impervious. (Alan)

Thus, for these three students, their emerging 'learning habitus' – a layer of habitus that is grafted onto their earlier habitus through the layering of new knowledge in practice – has taken place in relation to the doxic assumptions that they have experienced as gay men. Their life circumstances have positioned them uncomfortably within some social fields and they have already experienced a level of disruption in their social worlds. What is seen, therefore, in their self-reflective essays is the way their interaction with the module readings and discussions provided a productive space and theoretical frameworks that enabled them to begin to formulate their emerging 'teacherly becoming' in relation to their biographies.

"Being coloured is more a culture than a race"

The three PGCE students in this group identified the communities where they grew up as being characterised by "gangsterism, crime and a place where highly addictive drugs such as heroine and Tik (methamphetamine) are readily available" (Portia). Resisting the deficit positioning of these communities, these students discussed their biographies in relation to living in such communities. They lived in so-called coloured communities but attended schools elsewhere that were perceived to offer a better education. These students drew substantially on the work of Fataar (2015) where chapters describe, among other emphases, how students in the post-apartheid urban environment mediate racial and cultural differences as they travel across the city to access quality schooling. Fataar's book provided these students with an intellectual platform that enabled them to understand their own schooling experiences.

One of the PGCE students who attended primary school in her community but moved to a different area for high school describes her experience:

> At the time I felt greatly privileged to be part of what I believed to be superior schooling. Choosing to gain access to a remoter previously white school, my parents and I were oblivious to the positive and negative consequences of the choice. The change entailed longer school hours as well as longer days travelling to and from school ... These were surface issues in comparison to the fundamental impact on the construction of my identity. My alertness of being in a different environment was immediate due to the fact that I had only known my culture, my colour and my being (my reason for existing). I became acutely aware of my physical presence in the school as it was my first encounter with classmates of other races ... Suddenly I started questioning my intellectual abilities as I realised the standards were much higher than that of my previous school. Not only did I question my intellectual abilities, I also had to suppress my language style, topics of discussion amongst peers and cultural norms that I had taken for granted. (Jody)

The student here is describing the way in which discourses and practices operate in social spaces as a norm. She draws on Bourdieu (1990) who describes this as the doxa of a field or social space that operates as an underlying logic that dictates on a pre-verbal level the 'rules' of how social interactions take place in that particular field environment. Bourdieu (1990) also refers to this as the unwritten 'rules of the game'. In the excerpt above, Jody refers to a realisation that the rules of the game that she took for granted in her home and community environment were very different in the school environment she travelled to each day. She quickly realised that learning and adapting to these new rules was necessary for her to enjoy a relative sense of ease and success in the new school environment.

A second student similarly described her experiences of diversity and inclusivity within the high school she attended:

> The school embraced the changes of desegregation, not by their actions, but through hidden policies filed away behind locked doors. Through this it became apparent that I needed to assemble a new identity on the basis of my interaction between my race, language, culture and social standing and that of the school. Adopting the pre-existing culturally white ethos of the school became my new reality in order to make a success of my schooling career. (Chantel)

The three students who identify themselves as 'coloured' in their self-writing essays show how they have begun to reflexively draw on their own schooling experiences in relation to the readings and class discussion on diversity and inclusivity and their emerging 'teacherly becoming'. One of the students concludes her essay by saying:

> With regards to not recognising race (Fataar, 2015:70), I've myself experienced the effects thereof and will place an emphasis on the importance of acknowledging racial and cultural differences in my teaching environment ... I can begin to see how my past

has determined my current 'becoming' as a pre-service teacher and I have begun to see direct links between past events in my life and the current ways in which I navigate my pedagogy of teaching ... as such I want to conceptualise teaching as much more than just transferring knowledge to learners. (Jody)

"Born into democracy, born into the dream of Tata's rainbow nation"

The last group of students' self-writings that are discussed, are the students who identify as white middle-class students. They form the largest group of students who completed the reflective essays, not unexpected given the demographics of the PGCE cohort at Stellenbosch University. In their essays the students describe themselves as the "born-free generation" (Jana); "innocent and free from the mistakes of my white Afrikaans-speaking forefathers – or so I always believed" (Helene). Their narratives situate them in different social spaces in their life trajectories leading up to their PGCE studies at Stellenbosch University. However, central in each of their biographies is their recognition that despite being born post-1994, as suggested by Jansen's notion of inherited or indirect knowledge, "we all bear a part of our history in the pigmentation of our skin" (Lauren).

The students in this group describe their schooling years as a fairly easy existence, admitting that in most instances their "cultural capital ... closely coincided with that of the school" (Alison). They refer to an ease of transition from their homes and communities into their schooling where they found that their embodied cultural capital and habitus aligned with the requirements of the school system, allowing them access to the codes of schooling and consequently relative success in their educational endeavours. The students admit that the decision to study further after completing school was already inscribed in their habitus. One student notes that "my choice to go to university was based on my parents' expectations" (Michaela), while another states:

> I'm a third generation Matie. My parents and grandparents were in residences during their tertiary education. Before I walked into the residence I was known by the three generation of females that had gone before me. (Katherine)

As Jansen (2010) argues, forms of indirect knowledge exist in the students' 'knowledge in the blood', "knowledge that has long been routinised in how the second generation see the world and themselves, and how they understand others" (2010:171). It is the knowledge that is embedded in the "emotional, psychic, spiritual, social, economic, political, and psychological lives of a community" (Jansen, 2010:171).

Given this ease of privilege, most of these students acknowledge that it was only on arrival at university that they were exposed to ways in which they carried aspects of the past on their physical being. One student notes:

> It was only when I came to university that I really realised how I bear the pain of the past on my skin and in my language. My mere presence at university serves as a reminder of the unfair and discriminatory apartheid years and this hurts a large group of people … It is here at university where I have been exposed to the severity of how the past impacts on the future by way of my accepted assumptions that I have inherited through my family. (Helene)

Another student states:

> Through the journey of writing this essay I discovered the power of reflection. Reflecting on my own life story, how the experiences of my parents in the greater social context influenced the formation of my habitus. I had to reflect on how I deal with the shame I often experience when thinking of the past and still realising that the very thing I abhor still has power over my way of thinking. (Lauren)

Lauren's words powerfully provide evidence of how doxa, as a form of discourse and practice of certain beliefs and assumptions, continues to influence students' way of thinking and being. She draws on Bourdieu's concept of habitus in her reflections and further notes:

> The power of habitus in one's life is in its invisibility. When the invisible notions are brought to light, it creates an arena where the "embodied history internalized as second nature and so forgotten as history…" (Bourdieu in Panofsky, 2003:13) can be challenged. (Lauren)

The #FeesMustFall student protest movement erupted on university campuses while this group of students were at university. This movement was a student-led protest that began in October 2015 in response to an increase in fees at all South African universities. The protests started at the University of Witwatersrand and spread to other universities across the country. At the heart of the protests was the call for a decolonised free higher education for all students. The protest action at Stellenbosch University, led by a vocal and brave, yet relatively small, student group called Open Stellenbosch, called attention to the institution's exclusionary institutional culture. Capturing the attention of the university community, Open Stellenbosch played a key role in shifting the university's responses to a myriad of questions including language of instruction, residence culture, sexuality and gender parity. Open Stellenbosch was carefully monitored and contained by the university management; however, there were instances of violence and intimidation during the period of the protests in October 2015 and again in 2016. One student described a particular incident that took place while she was on her way to class during her final undergraduate year during the #FeesMustFall protests:

> Two students came up to me and started to push me around. They spat in my face and yelled, "You are a white supremacist and racist! You have privilege and have no idea what we, as people of colour, have been through!' To my shock it was two girls of my residence. That was the moment when I realised that, as an unintentional bearer of the past I am classified according to the colour of my skin and not by my humanity. I am seen as a white person ... who is unaware of their struggle ... my past creates my educational dilemmas (Nicole).

Another student notes how she came to realise the disjunction between how she was taught about the apartheid era in school and university, and how her family talked about the past:

> ... Over time I have come to realise that the same history that my family talks about with so much pride is based on injustice ... this has led to inner conflict about what my role in society should be as I feel guilty about my history and the privileges I have enjoyed ... In the module I began to make sense of this conflict ... reflecting on this I am finding a way forward where I can accept that my culture and language will always be part of me, but also realising that my skin, my language and the privilege I have enjoyed is also seen as an injustice by others. (Helene)

A central theme of the essays written by this group of students was their realisation, despite believing that they now lived in the post-1994 'rainbow nation', that as white students they were in actual fact still "carelessly carrying the hurt of discrimination and injustice on my skin" (Helene).

The complexity for the students of becoming aware of how the past has positioned them in relation to their 'becoming' as teachers is an important aspect that they navigate during their PGCE year. As stated by Dall'Alba (2009:34), learning professional ways of being – what she refers to as the "ambiguities of becoming" – involves not only what we know and can do, but also who we are (becoming). The self-writings of this group of students, as white middle-class pre-service teachers, show a struggle with aspects of this process in relation to the knowledge dimension of the readings and their knowing, acting and being. Most of this group of students close their essays by admitting that they are unsure how this awareness, the 'knowing' aspect of this process, can translate into practice; "the practical implications are still unknown to me and the challenge lies like a mountain before me" (Katherine).

Conclusion

The students' self-writings were submitted before they completed their compulsory twelve-week teaching practice in schools. The essays do not, therefore, show specific evidence of significant change in how they might enact their pedagogy as teachers one day. Rather, what the essays reveal is how as pre-service teachers their involvement in the class and tutorial discussions of the module History and Sociology of Education was beginning to frame their thinking in their 'becoming' as teachers. Earlier in this chapter we referred to the students' learning habitus as a form of secondary layering that becomes grafted over time on one's existing habitus. This relates to what Wacquant (2014:7) describes as a secondary layering that takes place "through specialized pedagogical labor". What the chapter suggests, therefore, is that for the students, the specialised pedagogical labour refers to their reflexive self-writing endeavours that have required them to "step back and gain distance from [their] dispositions" (Bourdieu & Wacquant, 1992:136), in order to reflect on how their social, cultural and educational backgrounds have shaped their view of the social world.

This chapter does not claim that the module's knowledge dimension, i.e. its intellectual focus, precipitated significant or transformative changes in the students' normative ways of thinking. While some shifts or changes might have taken place during the course of the module, the key argument of the chapter is that it was the students' reflexive engagement with the module readings and discussions in relation to their own biographies that supported the potential for them to begin to shift how they are thinking about themselves in relation to their emerging teacherly identity. The essays illustrated how their doxa of education was being challenged through their involvement in the module discussions. They show how, in and through this process, secondary habitus layers were being formed that have the potential to impact on, and shift and change, who they are becoming as pre-service teachers within the South African educational context. It is from this reflexive platform that the module goes on to concentrate on developing pedagogical approaches that would enable them to consider ways to engage their future learners in knowledge processes that involve rich and reflexive learning in schools. As part of the PGCE lecturing team, we have inserted the learnings developed in this module into the broader programme design, including the debriefing aspects of the professional placement school experience. The chapter thus contributes to ongoing programme design based on curriculum knowledge and pedagogical approaches that actively engender students' 'teacherly becoming' during their teacher education programme.

Acknowledgement

We wish to acknowledge the PGCE class for their generative lecture participation and essays which formed the basis for this chapter. A previous version of this chapter was published by the authors in the *South African Journal of Higher Education*, 2019, 33(6):133-152. https://doi.org/10.20853/33-6-3026

References

Bourdieu, P. 1977. *Outline of a theory of practice*. Cambridge: Cambridge University Press. https://doi.org/10.1017/CBO9780511812507

Bourdieu, P. 1990. *The logic of practice*. Stanford: Stanford University Press.

Bourdieu, P. & Eagleton, T. 1992. Doxa and common life. *Left Review*, 191(1):111-121.

Bourdieu, P. & Wacquant, L. 1992. *An invitation to reflexive sociology*. Great Britain: Polity Press.

Dall'Alba, G. 2009. Learning professional ways of being: Ambiguities of becoming. *Educational Philosophy and Theory*, 41:34-45. https://doi.org/10.1111/j.1469-5812.2008.00475.x

Department of Basic Education. 2014. *Curriculum Assessment Policy Statements*. South Africa. Available at: https://bit.ly/35FaZrC (accessed 12 January 2014).

Fataar, A. 2012. Mapping "teacherly becoming" on a teaching practice programme: A reflexive perspective. In: R. Osman & H. Venkat (eds), Research-led teacher education. Cape Town: Pearson, pp. 36-48.

Fataar, A. 2015. *Engaging schooling subjectivities across post-apartheid urban spaces*. Stellenbosch: African Sun Media. https://doi.org/10.18820/9781920689834

Feldman, J.A. & Fataar, A. 2019. Students' emerging pedagogical reflexivities in respect of their student teacherly becoming on a PGCE Diversity and Inclusivity module. *South African Journal of Higher Education*, 33(6):133-152. https://doi.org/10.20853/33-6-3026

Fraser, N. 1997. *Justice interruptus: Critical reflections on the "postsocialist" condition*. Cambridge: Cambridge University Press.

Jansen, J. 2010. *Knowledge in the Blood*. Stanford: Stanford University Press.

Maton, K. 2008. Habitus. In: M. Grenfell (ed.), *Pierre Bourdieu. Key concepts*. Durham: Acumen Publishing Limited, pp. 49-66. https://doi.org/10.1017/UPO9781844654031.006

Panofsky, C. 2003. The relations to learning and student social class: Toward "re-socializing" sociocultural learning theory. In: A. Kozulin, B. Gindis, V. Ageyev & A. Miller (eds), *Vygotsky's educational theory in cultural context*. Cambridge: Cambridge University Press, pp. 411-431. https://doi.org/10.1017/CBO9780511840975.021

Samuel, C. 2013. Symbolic violence and collective identity: Pierre Bourdieu and the ethics of resistance. *Social Movement Studies*, 12(4):397-414. https://doi.org/10.1080/14742837.2013.823345

Thompson, J. 1991. Introduction. In: J. Thompson (ed.), *Language and symbolic power*. Cambridge: Harvard University Press, pp. 1-15.

Thomson, I. 2004. Heidegger's perfectionist philosophy of education. *Being and Time*, 37:429-467. https://doi.org/10.1007/s11007-005-6886-8

Thomson, P. 2008. Field. In: M. Grenfell (ed), *Pierre Bourdieu: Key concepts*. Durham: Acumen Publishing Limited, pp. 65-80.

Wacquant, L. 2014. Homines in extremis: What fighting scholars teach us about habitus. *Body & Society*, 20(2):3-17. https://doi.org/10.1177/1357034X13501348

SECTION B
Deliberations within subject-specific modules

Teaching business ethics to pre-service teachers: An integrated approach

Carina America

Introduction

At the recent World Economic Forum event in Davos, Switzerland, the risks which climate change poses to the financial, environmental, and economic systems were again placed as the ethical and social responsibility of businesses and governments. Teenage activist Greta Thunberg's efforts to save the planet drew the attention of the socially conscious millennial generation worldwide (Bouw, 2020), including for her presentation at Davos. For more than a century, managers and global academic leaders perceived business education as being synonymous with the provision of a certain knowledge corpus that will enable individuals to acquire a global mind-set and achieve high corporate and self-performance levels (Anninos & Chytiris, 2011). However, the achievement of high-performance levels includes paying attention to ethics and other corporate responsibility issues, which depend on a way of thinking and acting beyond generally accepted business imperatives. Anninos and Chytiris

(2011) aver that unquestioned assumptions by management practitioners and scholars about the 'bottom line' culture have stripped business education of its ethical dimension. Brenkert (2010) argues that an ethical code for business is vital to counterweight profit maximisation and self-interest by balancing the way business managers act and approve policies, and the role companies play in society.

Professional ethics education has a long history in diverse fields such as medicine, law and business schools (Slocum, Rohlfer & Gonzales-Canton, 2014; Warnick & Silverman, 2011), and has shown that the practical relevance of ethics as a field of study is both crucial and longstanding. For example, a physician's ability and willingness to act in accordance with accepted moral norms and values are key components of professional behaviour. As a result, educational objectives relating to ethics are now often incorporated into broader goals for professionalism education (Carrese et al., 2015).

However, if our students and school learners are able to become citizens who hold governments and corporations accountable for their actions, then how we teach business ethics as part of Business Studies Teaching methodology becomes equally important, but it is also a challenge. There is limited coverage of business ethics at school level in the *Curriculum and Assessment Policy Statement* (CAPS) for Business Studies (see DBE, 2011). The coverage and time allocation is restrictive for such an important section of business content knowledge. Education has a pivotal role to sensitise students about the impact of business activities and decisions, not solely in terms of economic advancement, but also in terms of business's role towards environmental and societal stewardship (America, 2014). The challenge is the teachers' understandings of ethical predicaments in the business world and how that is being taught. For example, the future realisation of the sustainability of the earth's resources, economic welfare and society's well-being is undisputed, yet many business textbooks focus on the traditional business frameworks with the ultimate goal of profit maximisation (Maistry & David, 2018). Amidst the Covid-19 pandemic, 31 companies are being investigated for excessive price hikes (see SANews, 2020). How do educators acquire a teaching, learning and practical skill set for ethical awareness?

The attention given to ethics in undergraduate courses at university level is varied, coupled with a continuous struggle to give ethics its due weight to provide students with the knowledge, skills, and ethical sensitivity necessary for the world of work (Slocum et al., 2014). In most business programmes, undergraduate students receive very little organised formal education in business ethics, as this mostly occurs in postgraduate programmes (Desjardine, 2012). However, Glanzer and Ream (2007) and Warnick and Silverman (2011) reveal that certain professional majors, such as business, show a significant curricular attention to ethics, whereas a similar emphasis is not found in teacher education.

The issue of ethics in teacher education is mostly related to the professional ethics of teaching (Warnick & Silverman, 2011) – for example, practice teaching and the code of conduct for teachers – but less in the domain of the specialised disciplinary modules. Literature on ethics for initial teacher education is scant, particularly in business-related modules for teacher education such as the Business Studies Teaching module, which I teach to Postgraduate Certificate in Education (PGCE) students.

For the purpose of this study, I will refer to business ethics as: "a specialized study of moral right and wrong as they apply to business institutions, organizations and behaviour" (Velasquez, 2006:12). The moral right and wrong encompasses the virtues, values and standards that govern business or organisational decision-making.

A self-study methodology (see Van Laren, 2011; Zeichner, 2007) is undertaken to illustrate how two elements of the Productive Pedagogies framework (Lingard, Hayes & Mills, 2003) underpin the integration of business ethics in the PGCE teachers' programme. Business ethics as part of Business Studies Teaching methodology is a challenge, but a necessary one if our school students are to become citizens who hold governments and corporations accountable for their actions.

Locating the study

Slocum et al. (2014:46) found three main approaches to introducing ethics into a module: a stand-alone subject, a modular approach within a subject or a fully hybrid approach. A stand-alone business ethics course in a teacher education programme is unlikely because business modules are electives and will come with additional resource and opportunity costs. A modular approach is where business ethics content is taught as a specific part, for example for a week, and thereby constitutes an additional component of the subject matter. I apply a hybrid approach which is a continuous integrated approach, incorporating characteristics of both traditional and online classroom settings where learning occurs in both synchronous and asynchronous modes. Business ethics modules do not normally reside within education faculties, and it is up to the teacher educator to discern if and how a module of this nature should be integrated into the Business Studies Teaching module. The challenge is that there are no clear-cut guidelines or universal answers as to the specific ethics that should be taught to Business Teacher educators apart from the incorporation of one's pedagogy with the limited school curriculum content.

In the PGCE Business Studies Teaching module, students enter the programme with prerequisite disciplinary or content knowledge acquired in their bachelor's degrees. The *Minimum Requirements for Teaching Education Qualifications* (MRTEQ) stipulates five types of learning for initial teacher education: disciplinary, pedagogical, practical, fundamental, and situational learning (DHET, 2015). As qualified teachers, they work with two types of knowledge predominantly: disciplinary and pedagogical. Disciplinary knowledge is the powerful knowledge that should be prioritised because it allows students to move beyond their ordinary lives (Young & Muller, 2013:107). Young and Muller assert that "powerful knowledge is reliable knowledge that aims to achieve truth about the world we live in and what it is to be human that is nevertheless *always fallible and open to challenge*" (107). Hordern (2018) is of the view that the powerfulness proposed by Young and Muller is also dependent on certain socio-epistemic and institutional conditions. Ethical misdemeanours have become pervasive in our society and cut across the business sector, government institutions, higher education institutions and various parastatals. But as pointed out earlier, Business Studies Teaching curriculum content which relates to ethics is not as prevalent and most discussions around ethical indiscretions are reserved for outside of the classroom and in social settings. The pedagogical challenge is to live up to the powerfulness of disciplinary knowledge; to keep it relevant, interesting and let it resonates with students from diverse contexts.

Pedagogical learning incorporates general pedagogical knowledge and refers to the study of the principles, practices and methods of teaching (including knowledge of learners, learning, curriculum and general instructional and assessment strategies) and specialised pedagogical content knowledge. Pedagogical knowledge includes knowing how to present the concepts, methods, and rules of a specific discipline in order to create appropriate learning opportunities for diverse learners, and knowing how to evaluate their progress (DHET, 2011). Shulman (1986) also refers to this as 'pedagogical content knowledge' and notes that teachers need both disciplinary (business) knowledge and pedagogical content knowledge to teach effectively.

The PGCE programme at my institution is underpinned by the Productive Pedagogies framework which consists of four dimensions (Lingard et al., 2003): intellectual quality; connectedness; supportive classroom environment; and recognition of difference (Figure 7.1). The Productive Pedagogies framework originated as a large classroom-based research project undertaken in Australia.

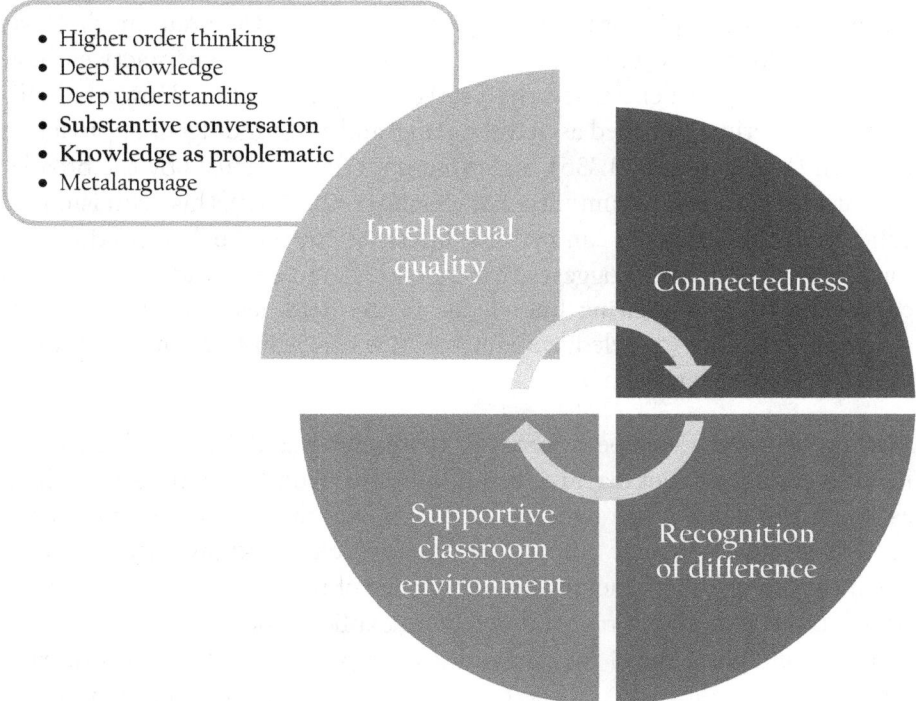

Figure 7.1 Productive Pedagogies framework for teacher education – thinking and planning around four principles (adapted from Lingard et al., 2003)

The purpose of this self-study is not to delve into all four of the dimensions, but rather to reflect on two elements of the intellectual quality dimension. Intellectual quality within the Productive Pedagogies framework refers to the higher-order thinking required of PGCE students to interrogate information and ideas in ways that transform their meaning and implications (Lingard et al., 2003). The two elements, namely, knowledge as problematic and substantive conversation, were selected as a focus of this study because of their potential to elicit critical discussion about contemporary business dilemmas. As the two dimensions become more prevalent in class, students can delve deeper into their own current perceptions which may then change over time.

Self-study methodology

Self-study broadly refers to a study based on a teacher educator's own practice, experience and action for reflection (Van Laren, 2011). The self-study research community is well established with marked focus on practitioner-generated knowledge about teacher education. This type of research sets out to create value for specific topics or to review particular issues (Cochran-Smith, Davis & Fries, 2004) as teacher educators' studies of their own practices have become more prevalent since the 1990s (Zeichner, 2007). However, self-study is sometimes labelled as 'navel-gazing' and a self-indulgent approach to research (Van Laren, 2011:336), and often not taken seriously by the broader educational research community. For Zeichner (2007:40), this criticism is of concern as the approach can make a difference "in the quality of education for teaching". Zeichner suggests that individual and case study research can contribute to accumulating knowledge in the field: learning through self-study to articulate knowledge about practice can manifest when self-study moves beyond the individual self.

Moving "beyond a recipe approach" to teaching and learning, self-study involves teaching about teaching that is linked to an understanding of teaching as being problematic (Loughran, 2005:9). Loughran maintains that in the process of "grasping" and "unpacking" the problematic knowledge of how to teach (teaching about teaching), a knowledge of teacher education practices begins to be recognised, responded to, and explicitly developed. In this self-study, I highlight some of the ambiguities and paradoxes of ethics education for Business Studies' pre-service teachers. I use Productive Pedagogies as a conceptual framework for my teaching, specifically as Slocum et al. (2014) suggest, to urge my students to pose questions, to think critically and to synthesise situational data and viewpoints in an integrated way, over time.

According to LaBoskey (2004), to legitimise the self-study methodology the research should be: self-initiated and self-focused; aimed at improvement; using multiple (mainly qualitative) methods; interactive at one or more stages of the process; and lastly, validated through the construction, testing, sharing and retesting of the exemplars of teaching practice. This self-study is therefore a hybrid approach to elicit ethical sensitivity based on two elements of the Productive Pedagogies framework: I contextualise the content through substantive conversation and confront (disciplinary) knowledge as problematic. Ethical considerations and being conscious of my integrity as a researcher were considered as I proceeded with the reflection of my practice. The reflection of my practice occurred through observation, journaling of my lectures and group discussions with thirty-five students over two years.

In Business Studies Teaching and teacher education, much depends on the teachers' own value propositions and ethical sensitivity. As Horden (2018) cautions, teachers need to understand that powerful knowledge is reliant on certain socio-epistemic and institutional conditions. In South Africa, the professional teacher qualification is based on MRTEQ, which encompasses broad learning principles for student teachers. However, the conditions within which powerful knowledge plays itself out are couched in a diverse, multilingual, and unequal (higher) educational environment. Business Teacher education is a field that functions at the interface of higher education and schooling, and therefore the complexity and context of the school system (in)directly impact on teacher education programmes (America & Le Grange, 2019). Moreover, in the case of teacher education, Brennan (2019) warns that unless educators are self-invested in knowledge about ethical issues of, for example, the environment, it is unlikely that a serious effort will be made to acquire proper understanding of the complex challenges local and global communities face.

I apply the five defining characteristics for self-study identified by LaBoskey (2004) to link the pedagogy of business ethics to the Productive Pedagogies framework that was adopted for the new PGCE programme, which started in 2018. As teacher educator, then, I present ethical dilemmas mainly in relation to the topics which deal with theories and principles of professionalism and ethics. I explore how these ethical aspects relate to the changing business environments and their application in practice.

First, I identify the need to have a more prominent focus on business ethics for teachers. I make the connection to the business environment, relating it to other themes in the curriculum (business operations: use of funds, abusing work time, misuse of resources, etc.). I incorporate real-life examples of how unethical business behaviour leads to corruption and deceit in the use of (government) resources. The state capture inquest in South Africa provides a mix of unethical examples including bribery, misuse of power for own ends, corrupt behaviour, capturing of state resources and irregularities with the issuing of tenders (see Business Day, 2019), which I incorporate in my classes.

Second, I focus on two aspects that fall under the intellectual quality dimension, specifically, 'substantive conversation' and 'knowledge as problematic' to elicit critical thinking aimed at improvement. Business ethics for teacher education does not necessarily focus on the students' personal value systems, but rather leads them to self-understanding (Sims & Felton, 2006) and to deepen their experiential awareness of ethical dilemmas particularly in diverse settings.

Third, I use multiple methods, such as curriculum analysis, case study analysis and reflection on lesson analysis. Dion (2015:110) highlights three levels at which ethical issues arise: macro (business and society), meso (intra-organisational and inter-organisational levels), and micro (intrapersonal and interpersonal levels). Through case studies, business articles and newspaper clippings, I continuously integrate, discuss, and compare the ethics and inner morality of the market (macro level), the ethics of social institutions (meso level), and the ethics of organisations (micro level) as they would interact with personal value systems (Block & Cwik, 2007). By integrating the resource material (e.g. analysis of a case study) and the students' existing powerful knowledge, I integrate three basic questions asked by Gandz and Hayes (1988:666), which are still relevant today:

- Who will be affected by this decision that you are about to make?
- How will each party or stakeholder identified by you, be affected?
- How do the answers to the two questions above impact on society and the environment?

When students answer these questions, they will be guided to their decision in terms of the objectives they want to meet regarding the ethical dilemma presented. I also prompt them to seek alternatives to their perspectives and consider how their decisions can be implemented for the betterment of society and the environment.

Fourth, I changed the focus of the PGCE module to a continuous integration of ethical issues by using the theoretical underpinning of the Productive Pedagogies framework. The reflective questions above allow students' virtues, values, and standards to come to the fore – aspects which otherwise may not have been brought out by the problematic case or scenario presented.

Lastly, teaching practice must illustrate a deliberate attempt where students share and integrate activities related to ethics. Integration of substantive conversations and creation of a space where knowledge can be disrupted are used to illustrate a mind-shift of the pre-service teachers, which was evident in their lessons during teaching practice. Focusing on ethical dilemmas may make both teacher educators and students uncomfortable which imply that I had to take risks (see Loughran, 2005). I also recognise that I can reinvent myself as a teacher educator by continuously interrogating my own practice and any preconceived notions I may have had.

Knowledge as problematic and substantive conversation in PGCE Business Studies Teaching

All knowledge should be problematic and recognised as socially constructed. Knowledge should therefore not be presented as given because it then represents the subject content as an unchallengeable fact. In Business Studies Teaching, in certain cases, knowledge can appear static when presented in tables, charts and textbooks. However, the discussion around the interpretation of static knowledge can be fluid and problematic.

My engagement with the *knowledge as problematic* aspect of the Productive Pedagogies framework takes the form of creating a welcoming atmosphere in my lectures where students are encouraged to be open and frank without feeling restricted or self-conscious. I specifically welcome and explore multiple contrasting and potentially conflicting opinions, nudging my students to critically examine the scenarios under discussion. I highlight some of the paradoxes and disparities in how the business world functions, elicit curiosity, engagement and critique with the aim of robust discussion and self-reflection on the part of the students.

Still today, the traditional neo-classical underpinning of business continues to stand firm: profit maximisation, competitiveness and shareholder wealth remain the cornerstone of business activity. So, when Apple (2001) argues that it is justifiable when parents are concerned about their children's future, it is because the neoliberal business is notorious for putting profit before people and the environment.

Substantive conversation means that the interaction in class is thoughtful, reciprocal and promotes a common understanding. This kind of conversation is rooted in reality, and the exchange is meaningful and constructive. The idea is a reciprocal and sustained dialogue between the students and I, and amongst the students themselves. Talking about ethical conduct can be awkward, problematic and complicated, and could disrupt traditional ways of thinking about the business world, content knowledge and the curriculum. Essentially, I create a safe space where students feel comfortable with uncomfortable and difficult conversations. Substantive conversations reveal important tensions in the classroom, where autonomous and critical thinking are encouraged, and where these opinions can be voiced confidently. I integrate business ethics throughout the curriculum by following three features as part of substantive conversation as clarified by the Productive Pedagogies framework:

- *Intellectual substance* encourages critical reasoning with regard not only to subject matter, but also to pedagogy and assessment. This includes making distinctions, applying ideas, forming generalisations, and raising questions. Sometimes I would also include fictitious scenarios from the macro, meso and micro-environments if I cannot find a real-life illustration, e.g. the agency problem which refers to conflict of interest in a particular relationship and where one party acts in his own interest, without taking the other party's interest into account (see Masson, Tibault & Misener, 2006). Professional codes of conduct are used to guide discussions, ultimately encouraging students to think as autonomous moral agents.

- *Dialogue and sustained exchange* are promoted where conversations include the sharing of ideas; this is reciprocal as opposed to lecturer-led narrations or presentations. Business Studies Teaching PGCE students enter this course with substantial disciplinary knowledge acquired in their bachelor's degrees, in some instances with work experience. The students extend our conversations and raise questions, coming from their own experiences. This also leads to sustained exchanges where discussions are prompted by our previous conversations, and new connections are made about topical issues. For example, the state capture inquiry brought about heated discussion around the professional and ethical conduct of ex-president Zuma and his involvement in the case. Students started asking questions about their rights as taxpayers, consumers, and citizens.

  In contrast to a theoretical approach to the teaching of ethics, I use case discussions and scenario-mapping of ethical dilemmas in my classes. In these discussions, I look at the merits and demerits of the ethical dilemma and its moral implications. We explore plausible ways of implementation or means of solving a problem. By using case analysis, I allow my students to develop what Strike (1993:105) terms dialogical competence: "the ability to talk about, reason about, and experience appropriate phenomena via a certain set of concepts". Warnick and Silverman (2011) suggest that teachers need to offer some hope that an intelligent and principled resolution of ethical dilemmas is possible, but at the same time challenge students to reject the teacher's authority in simply giving them these resolutions. In this way, I encourage open-ended ethical inquiry as opposed to what Warnick and Silverman (2011:276) refer to as a "procedural view of objectivity" in ethics.

- *Logical extension and synthesis* are integrated as a follow-up on dialogue and sustained exchange. My synthesis of class conversations is always linked to the topics in the curriculum. The process I follow involves a framework using the different elements of ethics codes, e.g. the incorporation of the King Code of Corporate Governance (King Committee on Corporate Governance and Institute of Directors, 2002) and a business's code of conduct. These elements help ease the pedagogical tension between promoting moral autonomy and maintaining the possibility of moral objectivity. My lectures take the form of a properly constructed process where students critically examine texts, ideas and knowledge, and whilst I am open to differing student suppositions, I also do not give the impression that 'anything goes' or that ethics is only about subjective opinion. In consolidating the discussions, the following questions are put to the students:

- How do each of your opinions about solving the problem impact on the dilemma presented? Most students welcomed the diverse responses to scenarios, and many were influenced by the discussions in the class compared to their initial response to the ethical dilemma presented. Comments included: "I haven't looked at it in that way …", or "I wish someone can teach government cabinet ministers a course in ethics and professionalism before they are appointed".
- Do you see yourself as an important stakeholder in society? Do you think stakeholders in this case/scenario/dilemma are being treated fairly? If you were a stakeholder in this instance, how would you like to be treated? All the students felt that they matter. They would like to be treated fairly and consider that their human rights should not be violated. Comments like: "… we should be more vocal as consumers and voters to corruption…" and: "Many of our people are poor and illiterate, so businesses can take advantage of them for their own interest".
- Are ethical and moral codes relevant in this scenario and how can they remedy the situation? The students appreciated the values clarification of professional and ethical codes of conduct which were integrated in the group discussions. They could extract what was relevant to a specific scenario and some referred to "the King Code of Corporate Governance as an important code of ethics to keep businesses in check". Other students felt that the financial crisis of 2008 had not had much impact on "the greed of big business".

My self-reflection was a meaningful way to uncover several assertions made by Loughran (2005) and Van Laren (2011) when they refer to the ultimate transformative nature of the self-study process. In addition, some of the basic goals for ethical sensitivity by Felton and Sims (2005) resonate with a continuous integrated approach to ethics teaching in the PGCE Business Studies module. I will explain, by means of four key aspects, how my process unfolded and led to the outcomes (see Figure 7.2).

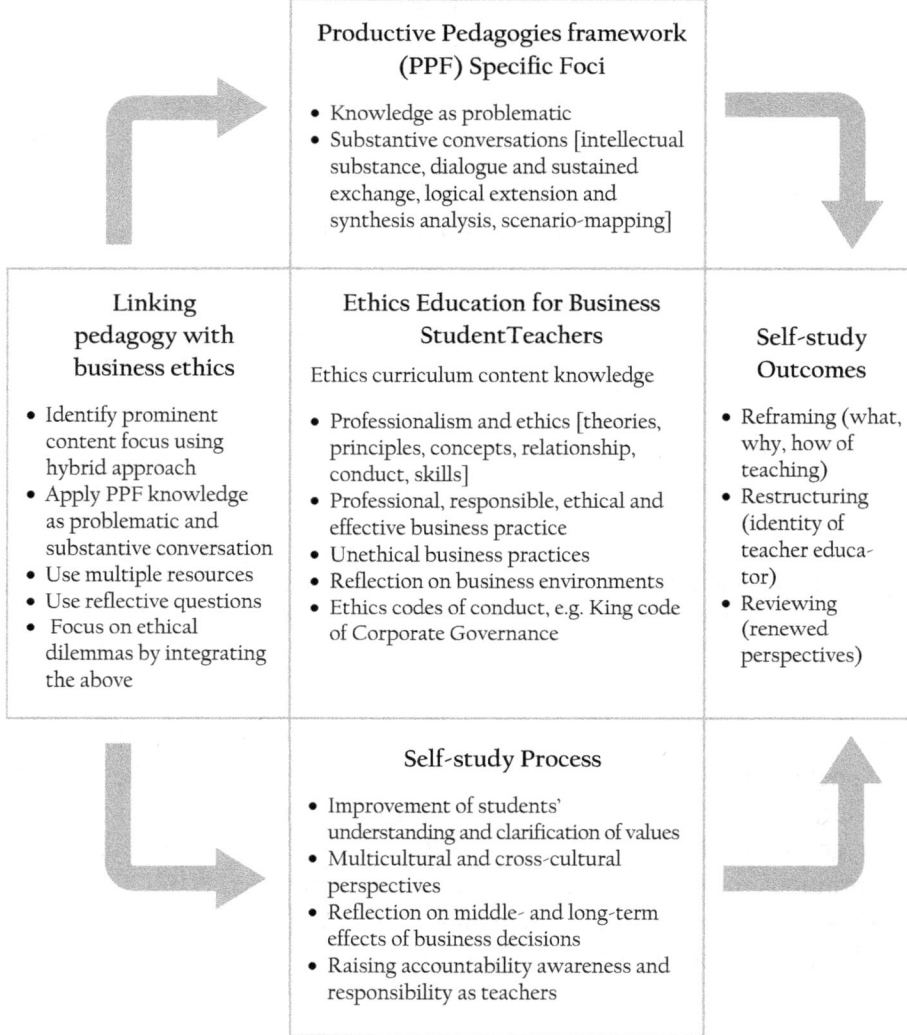

Figure 7.2 Business ethics framework for Business Teacher education

First, I saw improvement in the students' understanding and clarification of their own values. Some students admitted to being prejudiced initially by long held beliefs and stereotypes. Students realise that being professional is not enough; professionalism is important but it does not presuppose ethical conduct. The students showed a broader understanding of this and how ethics is embedded in Business Studies. I could therefore apply general awareness raising of contemporary ethical issues. For example, deliberations on current exposure of corruption within government parastatals such as the Passenger Rail Agency of South Africa (PRASA), the Electricity Supply

Commission (ESKOM), South African Airways (SAA) and others were welcomed in class discussions. This kind of consciousness is ongoing in my pedagogic approaches and interrogation of the content prescribed in the curriculum. I deliberately integrate the critical questions referred to earlier to create an enduring ethical sensitivity among students. I elicit deeper thinking of business's responsibilities toward all stakeholders, by the ethical awareness of the implication (and undermining) of scarcities and sustainable resource production in the supply chain. We focus on the ecological impact in the global arena (for example, climate change, the depletion of the ozone layer, threats to marine ecosystems) and how these developments shape the mindsets of students and educators. For example, the expanded view of the triple bottom line is part of my pedagogy for ethical awareness; this view moves beyond mere social, economic and environmental resilience in the business sector, to create a symbiotic relationship between natural, human, socially-manufactured and financial capital. Teachers can have an impact on how young learners become self-aware and conscious of the consequences of their own behaviour as current and future consumers, which could then become transformative (America, 2014). For example, consumers have the power to refrain from buying goods that are detrimental to society and the environment. In so doing, they put pressure on businesses to produce products which are environmentally friendly and of enduring value.

Second, I adopted a multicultural/cross-cultural perspective. I follow the path of inter-culturality to explicitly model contextualised teaching. This is an active process of unlearning and re-learning, highlighting integrated relationships between persons or social groups of diverse worldviews and cultures. This understanding mitigates students' preconceived notions that ethical misconduct may be more prevalent in certain groups than others. I consciously use case studies that reflect a diverse range of businesses, e.g. multinationals, local businesses and those from other African countries. Although African business case studies are not as freely accessible as cases in the broader business education world (America & Le Grange, 2019), it is important that business student teachers are aware of business operations on the African continent.

Third, I helped the students to explore the middle- and long-term effects of managerial decisions (Felton & Sims, 2005). Corporations are the primary agents of economic development. How they leverage ecological solutions in the face of economic and technological advancements, for example, is therefore crucial. My role was to anticipate divergent views on, for example, issues around the ethics of resource extraction (for example, fracking) and enquiries around the latest developments in the media. I facilitate discussions through ethical and moral questioning: What does it mean for a business to have ecological integrity? How do businesses show respect and care for the community? Do you stay silent if a business infringes on the social and economic justice of a community? How do you respond if fair trade, sustainable resource use, environmental protection and progressive labour standards are infringed? I also encourage students to interrogate and contest the content presented in textbooks, e.g. the relativism of the notion of professionalism across cultures where dress codes differ and business conduct varies. This normally takes the form of asking critical questions and contextualising my teaching. It requires a change of mind and emotion on the part of the students when they realise their interdependence and individual efforts are needed to keep businesses accountable. This is a mindset that can be trickled down to school level.

Fourth, I raised students' awareness of the accountability and responsibility that comes with being teachers and educators. My role is to help students understand and uncover the interconnectedness between personal values and the business/institutional/organisational and even educational values. A personal value may include being aware of the possible exploitation of consumers in South Africa (see SANews, 2020), a country where many people are not financially literate. A considerable part of the population does not have access to consumer education or financial literacy resources and lacks sufficient knowledge to make informed decisions about products offered to consumers, e.g. taking out insurance or opening a bank account. The Business Studies class should be seen from the perspective of different stakeholders and their obligations, e.g. making students aware of the role of 'watchdog' organisations such as the Consumer Association, the South African Insurance Association (SAIA) and the King Code of Corporate Governance (King Committee on Corporate Governance and Institute on Directors, 2002). Many of my student teachers realised that the power bestowed upon teachers is immense and their actions and ideologies can have a lasting impact on learners. What is learnt today can shape behaviour of tomorrow. Cultivating the skills to develop ethical sensitivity and moral courage cannot be sooner than at school level. This opportunity comes with risks and discomfort in confronting awkward issues that are often 'swept under the carpet' in typical class discussions.

Loughran (2004:18) avers: "Self-study defines the focus of study and not the way the study is carried out". The responsibility is therefore on myself as a researcher to justify my approach in relation to the desired outcomes of reframing, restructuring, and renewing (Van Laren, 2011). These outcomes are explained briefly as follows:

- *Reframing* refers to my reflection on what, why and how I was teaching. Through this self-study I realised the value of disrupting (existing) knowledge, asking uncomfortable questions and allowing substantive conversations to flow. My approach to teaching has taken a turn towards more real-world difficult scenarios in my classes.
- *Restructuring* is a deliberate shift to my identity as a business teacher educator and the focus on my students' teaching and learning of Business Studies instead of focusing on the context in which the students are situated. I flipped my lectures around so that all of us are dependent on one another for the lesson. All our views are important; not only mine as the educator. This restructuring worked well with the diversity in my classes. Students can bring their own experiences and (indigenous) knowledge systems to discussion. I realised that I function well in a less rigid, open-ended, yet objective role.
- *Renewing* enabled a fresh look at my past experiences and actions as a Business Education Teacher educator and expansion of pedagogical content knowledge integrated with contemporary issues and its relation to ethical awareness.

The reframing, restructuring, and renewing refer to my integration process, my discernment of what content is considered the most impactful and how it should be taught.

Conclusion

Excellence in the business world means more than merely having business acumen; it also presupposes a broad education that includes ethical integrity and virtuous behaviour in a business environment. However, in real life, having moral and ethical conduct are not necessarily treated as one of the core functions of a business. Often, Business Studies Teacher educators are not critical about the capacity of formal curriculum to mediate learning that raises questions about the conduct and decision-making of corporate businesses. The challenge for business teacher educators is that they do not teach the managers of the future; instead, they teach pre-service teachers to think ethically so that ethical sensitivity can be cascaded down to school level. The teaching of business ethics and its implementation (action) is therefore challenging, as student teachers are not actually going into the field to act on it although their learners might. Students, as citizens, need ways to think about what appropriate ethical conduct in business in a country is where corruption is experienced all too often. The pedagogical challenges of dealing with teaching business ethics is that this is a long and continuous process which requires patience from the teacher educator to facilitate substantive conversations. Arising in this study was a (re)new way of thinking about how ethical conduct by business plays out in society and how it is being taught in a constructive way.

Through self-study I have explored how substantive conversations and treating knowledge as problematic can give credence to integrating business ethics in teacher education. In so doing, moral and ethical sensitivities could have an elevated function for business teacher educators. The responsibility lies not only with business education but also within business teacher education, as argued in this reflection.

References

America, C. 2014. Integrating sustainability into business education teacher training. *South African Journal of Education*, 34(3):1-8. https://doi.org/10.15700/201409161105

America, C. & Le Grange, L. 2019. Dekolonisering van die kurrikulum: 'n kontekstualisering van Ekonomie- en Besigheidstudieonderrig/Decolonising the curriculum: contextualising Economics and Business Studies teaching. *Tydskrif vir Geesteswetenskappe*, 59(1):106-123. https://doi.org/10.17159/2224-7912/2019/v59n1a7

Anninos, L.N. & Chytiris, L. 2011. Searching for excellence in business education. *Journal of Management Development*, 30(9):882-892. https://doi.org/10.1108/02621711111164358

Apple, M.W. 2001. Comparing neo-liberal projects and inequality in education. *Comparative Education*, 37(4):409-423. https://doi.org/10.1080/03050060120091229

Block, W. & Cwik, P.F. 2007. Teaching business ethics: A 'classificationist' approach. *Business Ethics: a European Review*, 16(2):98-107. https://doi.org/10.1111/j.1467-8608.2007.00480.x

Bouw, B. 2020. *Making money work for you—and the planet: Younger investors are demanding their investments be a force for good, and big finance is listening.* Toronto: Rogers Media Inc.

Brenkert, G.G. 2010. The limits and prospects of business ethics. *Business Ethics Quarterly*, 20(4):703-709. https://doi.org/10.5840/beq201020444

Brennan, M. 2019. Changing teaching and teacher education in the 'Anthropocene'. *Journal of Research and Debate*, 2(4):1-6.

Business Day, 2019. Five highlights of the state capture accusations in 2019. Available at: https://bit.ly/3lY1cmx [accessed 3 May 2020].

Carrese, J.A., Malek, J., Watson, K., Lehmann, L.S., Green, M.J., McCullough, L.B., Geller, G., Braddock III, C.H. & Doukas, D.J. 2015. The essential role of medical ethics education in achieving professionalism: The Romanell Report. *Academic Medicine*, 90(6):744-752. https://doi.org/10.1097/ACM.0000000000000715

Cochran-Smith, M., Davis, D. & Fries, K. 2004. Multicultural teacher education: Research, practice, and policy. In: J. Banks (ed.), *Handbook of research on multicultural education.* 3rd Edition. San Francisco: Jossey-Bass, pp. 931-975.

Desjardine, M. 2012. Making the right decision: Incorporating ethics into business education. *Teaching Innovation Projects*, 2(1):6.

Dion, M. 2015. Epistemological and pedagogical challenges of teaching international business ethics courses. *Journal of Teaching in International Business*, 26(2):109-135. https://doi.org/10.1080/08975930.2015.1038416

DBE (Department of Basic Education). 2011. *Curriculum and Assessment Policy Statement Grades 10–12: Business Studies.* Pretoria, South Africa. Government Press.

DHET (Department of Higher Education and Training). 2015. *Revised policy on the minimum requirements for teacher education qualifications.* Government Gazette No 38487. Pretoria, South Africa: Department of Higher Education and Training.

Felton, E.L. & Sims, R. 2005. Teaching business ethics: Targeted outputs. *Journal of Business Ethics*, 60(4):377-391. https://doi.org/10.1007/s10551-004-8206-3

Gandz, J. & Hayes, N. 1988. Teaching business ethics. *Journal of Business Ethics*, 7(9):657-669. https://doi.org/10.1007/BF00382975

Glanzer, P.L. & Ream, T.C. 2007. Has teacher education missed out on the "ethics boom"? A comparative study of ethics requirements and courses in professional majors of Christian colleges and universities. *Christian Higher Education*, 6(4):271-288. https://doi.org/10.1080/15363750701268277

Hordern, J. 2018. Is powerful educational knowledge possible? *Cambridge Journal of Education*, 48(6):787-802.

King Committee on Corporate Governance and Institute of Directors (South Africa), 2002. *King report on corporate governance for South Africa, 2002*. Institute of Directors in Southern Africa.

LaBoskey, V.K. 2004. The methodology of self-study as its theoretical underpinnings. In: J.J. Loughran, M.L. Hamilton, V.K. LaBoskey & T. Russell (eds), *International handbook of self-study of teaching and teacher education practices*. Dordrecht: Kluwer Academic, pp. 817-869. https://doi.org/10.1007/978-1-4020-6545-3_21

Lingard, B., Hayes, D. & Mills, M. 2003. Teachers and Productive Pedagogies: Contextualising, conceptualising, utilising. *Pedagogy, Culture & Society*, 11(3):399-424. https://doi.org/10.1080/14681360300200181

Loughran, J.J. 2004. A history and context of self-study of teacher and teacher education practices. In: J.J. Loughran, M.L. Hamilton, V.K. LaBoskey & T. Russell (eds), *International handbook of self-study of teaching and teacher education practices*. Dordrecht: Kluwer Academic, pp. 7-39. https://doi.org/10.1007/978-1-4020-6545-3_1

Loughran, J. 2005. Researching teaching about teaching: Self-study of teacher education practices. *Studying Teacher Education*, 1(1):5-16. https://doi.org/10.1080/17425960500039777

Maistry, S.M. & David, R. 2018. The school economics textbook as programmatic curriculum: An exploited conduit for the neoliberal globalisation discourses. *Journal of Education*, 74:32-46. https://doi.org/10.17159/2520-9868/i74a03

Shulman, L.S. 1986. Those who understand knowledge growth in teaching. *Educational Researcher*, 15:4-14. https://doi.org/10.3102/0013189X015002004

Sims, R.R. & Felton, E.L. 2006. Designing and delivering business ethics teaching and learning. *Journal of Business Ethics*, 63(3):297-312. https://doi.org/10.1007/s10551-005-3562-1

Slocum, A., Rohlfer, S. & Gonzalez-Canton, C. 2014. Teaching business ethics through strategically integrated micro-insertions. *Journal of Business Ethics*, 125(1):45-58. https://doi.org/10.1007/s10551-013-1905-x

SANews (South African Government News Agency). 2020. Thirty companies investigated for excessive price hikes. Available at: https://bit.ly/2Hfvv8V [accessed 23 April 2020].

Strike, K.A. 1993. Teaching ethical reasoning using cases. In: K.A. Strike & P.L. Ternasky (eds), *Ethics for professionals in education: Perspectives for preparation and practice*. New York, NY: Teachers College Press, pp. 102-116.

Van Laren, L. 2011. Integrating HIV & Aids education in pre-service Mathematics Education for social justice. *South African Journal of Education*, 31(3):333-344. https://doi.org/10.15700/saje.v31n3a539

Velasquez, M.G. 2006. *Business ethics: Concepts and cases.* 6th Edition. Upper Saddle Creek, NJ: Pearson Education.

Warnick, B.R. & Silverman, S.K. 2011. A framework for professional ethics courses in teacher education. *Journal of Teacher Education*, 62(3):273-285. https://doi.org/10.1177/0022487110398002

Young, M. & Muller, J. 2013. On the powers of powerful knowledge. *Review of Education*, 1(3):229-250. https://doi.org/10.1002/rev3.3017

Zeichner, K. 2007. Accumulating knowledge across Self-Studies in Teacher Education. *Journal of Teacher Education*, 58(1):36-46. https://doi.org/10.1177/0022487106296219

Exploring pre-service science teachers' epistemic agency to develop their pedagogy for science teaching

Nazeem Edwards

Introduction

According to the Collins English dictionary, science is defined as: "The systematic study of the nature and behaviour of the material and physical universe, based on observation, experiment, and measurement, and the formulation of laws to describe these facts in general terms".[1] Scientists have established this body of scientific knowledge, but we say it is tentative because it can change as new discoveries are made which add to the body of knowledge. Thus, when learners engage in experimentation and measurement at school level, they are verifying the laws that scientists have already proven. For example, an investigation of the relationship between acceleration and the net force experienced by a body in motion would be a verification of one aspect of Newton's Second Law of motion. At best, the learners are acquiring

---

1   https://bit.ly/2UTGWGN

process skills in scientific investigation and should be able to formulate the law mathematically and in words. There are multiple ways in which the law can be represented that are appropriate to learners' needs (Ainsworth, 2008). There are many semiotic tools in language, algebraic systems, diagrams, etc. that are used for the appropriation of knowledge through representational activity (John-Steiner & Mahn, 1996).

My focus as a science teacher educator is to develop the pedagogical repertoire of pre-service science teachers in the Postgraduate Certificate in Education (PGCE) programme at university. This is underpinned by an epistemological question: How do the students come to know what they know in science? I proffer that they become enculturated into scientific discourse through interaction with experienced others who use the tools of established scientific practice. The students are graduates who have completed a minimum of three years specialising in Chemistry or Physics. This exposure to develop their disciplinary knowledge primarily occurs through engagement with the theory and practical work in the laboratory. Specialists in the discipline mediate these interactions, and as Rau (2017:724) stated: "These social interactions mediate students' engagement in both sense-making processes and inductive learning processes". Hordern (2015) also advanced the argument that, in teaching, improvements in educational outcomes can only be attained through sustained efforts by the professional community of teachers and teacher educators. This implies that there must be collaboration within a community of practice to realise these outcomes.

In this chapter, I argue that as a teacher educator in science education, my role is to introduce prospective science teachers into science-as-practice to develop them as epistemic agents in the classroom. I use sociocultural theory as a theoretical lens to understand how PGCE students develop their knowledge base for professional practice. As graduates, they have acquired the disciplinary knowledge in Physics and Chemistry, but appropriating the vertical discourse and recontextualising it for teaching is not an easy matter (Hordern, 2015). The prospective science teacher needs the pedagogical knowledge for teaching, which brings together the disciplinary discourses and the educational research that relates to pedagogy. In this respect, I outline how multiple representations are used as a pedagogic approach in the classroom to mediate scientific knowledge.

Sociocultural theory and science education

Leach and Scott (2003) posited that the goal of teaching is to introduce new ways of thinking and talking to students by showing how it is done in a particular context. They proposed that Vygotskian theory brings together the social plane and individual constructivism in regarding the student not as a tabula rasa, but as an active participant in the learning process. Students have to understand scientific knowledge and internalise it for their own personal use, and language plays an important role in mediating this knowledge. This sociocultural view of learning highlights the interdependence between the individual and social processes in learning and development (Scott & Palincsar, 2013).

Sociocultural theory shifts us away from transmission modes of pedagogy and opens up new possibilities for teaching and learning in the classroom (Daniels, 2001). The emphasis is on semiotic mediation as an explicit type to understand how higher mental processes function in the social world. Wertsch (2007) argued that Vygotsky emphasised qualitative transformation through the inclusion of signs and tools. He differentiates between implicit and explicit mediation as follows:

- Explicit mediation is when an overt and intentional stimulus is introduced into an activity, and the signs involved are obvious and non-transitory. The signs are usually designed by an external agent to help reorganise the activity.
- Implicit mediation is ephemeral, short-lived and less easily taken as an object of conscious reflection. It is not intentionally introduced into human action and becomes integrated with other forms of goal-directed behaviour. It "involves signs in the form of natural language that have evolved in the service of communication" (Wertsch, 2007: 185).

The zone of proximal development (ZPD) is a characteristic of sociocultural theory, and a notion extensively applied in education. It denotes the distance between what an individual could accomplish independently and in collaboration with others (Vygotsky, 1978:86). This has implications for the way in which a science lesson is designed and the facilitator role that the teacher can potentially play in the classroom to promote higher-order thinking. An example of this could be that learners are expected to observe what happens when water boils in a beaker. At a macroscopic level, they may state that steam is forming when the water boils. However, when they are challenged to explain this change of phase from a liquid to vapour, they may delve into the microscopic level and explain that heat increased the kinetic energy of the molecules, thereby causing the molecules at the surface to escape faster. This shows that in the absence of a prompt the learners would engage in surface learning rather than deep learning. It is also an example of scaffolding, which entails the novice being assisted by the experienced other in the social setting (Daniels, 2001). Depending on the level of education, what appears to be a simple explanation could evolve into something more complex when mathematical symbols and equations are introduced to represent the phase changes.

In science teacher education, the pedagogies that prospective science teachers appropriate are shaped within social settings. As Vygotsky (1978:55) stated: "The internalization of socially rooted and historically developed activities is the distinguishing feature of human psychology". Van der Veer (2007) also suggested that the shaping of abilities takes place in a specific sociocultural context, and individuals make use of the ideas and tools that are available. This is particularly important in science teaching, as the goal should be to support students to engage in activities and use the tools consistent with the practices of the community (Scott & Palincsar, 2013).

It is these semiotic tools that are a feature of multiple representations in science education, and which are used for explicit mediation purposes. I now briefly outline how these multiple representations are used in science education.

Multiple representations as explicit mediation

Multiple representations refer to the practice of re-representing the same concept through different forms. They are artefacts that symbolize an idea or concept in science (Prain & Waldrip, 2006; Tang, Degado & Moje, 2014). These can take the form of analogies, verbal explanations, written texts, diagrams, graphs and simulations. Research has also shown that student-generated representations can enhance learning (Waldrip & Prain, 2012). However, if they fail to see the interrelationships between the multiple representations then it could hinder their learning (Rau, 2020).

Multiple representations also help to connect various aspects of a phenomenon to build a deeper understanding (Won, Yoon & Treagust, 2014). Figure 9.1 illustrates diagrammatically how water undergoes a phase change that includes the symbolic as well as textual description. The diagram also shows the microscopic level to elucidate that the molecules are increasingly further apart as the temperature increases. This ties in with the ZPD as discussed above – the teacher can explore the concept at varying levels of complexity. Students, therefore, need to be able to translate from one representation to another and teachers should support such integration (Won et al., 2014:842). Moore et al. (2018) underscore this when they indicate that having a large repertoire of representations is inadequate unless teachers know how to scaffold students' ability to translate between representations.

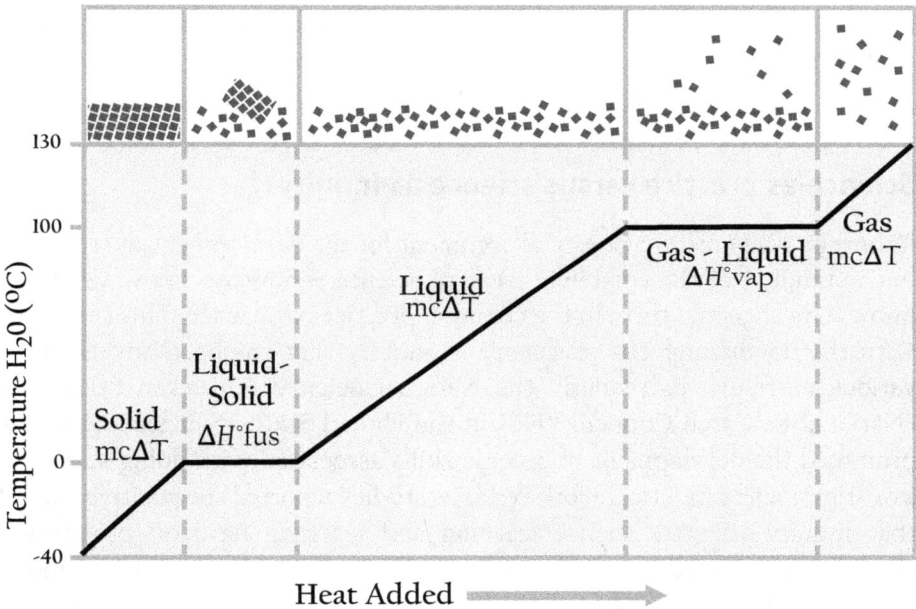

Figure 9.1 Phase changes of water

Kozma and Russell (2005) maintained that individuals use representational systems as they are integrated into communities of practice. This sociocultural perspective posits that representational competence is used to construct and communicate understanding. Again, this can be connected to the students' ZPD – those with little representational competence are likely to engage in surface learning while deep learning is more likely to occur when the student is able to navigate between different representations.

Rau (2017) also contended that when students acquire representational competence they become part of the science community of practice. It is through social interactions that they engage in disciplinary discourse which involves both verbal and non-verbal communication (Rau, 2017:724). In chemistry, for example, students have to visualise the formation of a chemical bond such as in the water molecule. This could be represented in various ways such as a Lewis diagram or a ball-and-stick model. Rau (2017:748) stated that different "representational competencies are a critical aspect of expert practices in chemistry". It is therefore important that students acquire this competence to make sense of different concepts in chemistry, and thus become enculturated to participate in scientific discourse (Rau, 2020).

In the next section, I outline what is meant by science-as-practice as a goal for PGCE students to develop their epistemic agency in the classroom. This is contrasted with science as inquiry, which is also a commonly supported goal in science.

Science-as-practice versus science-as-inquiry

Osborne (2014) made a powerful argument for the development of students' understanding of the epistemic basis of science – how we know what we know – by engaging them in the common practices of science. This contrasts with the dominant focus of science as inquiry that has been advanced by various curricula, particularly the National Science Education Standards (National Research Council, 1996) in the United States. Science-as-inquiry promoted the development of process skills associated with doing scientific investigations or practical work. Various studies reported the positive effects that inquiry-oriented science learning and teaching have on pre-service teachers' understanding of the nature of science, attitudes and beliefs about science learning and teaching, and their classroom teaching performance (Haefner & Zembal-Saul, 2004; Liang & Richardson, 2009). A Google Scholar search on process skills in science yields over five million hits in under one second. It is clear that there is no shortage of research on the topic and the research cited here is but a drop in the ocean. Research over the last twenty years has therefore strongly advocated for science-as-inquiry as the dominant pedagogical approach in the classroom.

Erduran and Dagher (2014) stated that school science has been dominated by an emphasis on teaching scientific processes with a focus on process skills. However, they argued that this fails to address how school science fits into wider scientific practices, which situate science into epistemic practices to develop scientific knowledge. This highlights the importance of scientific practices that are embedded in social and cultural practices, and consequently promotes the acquisition of epistemic knowledge in science. The National Research Council (2012:50-53) elaborated on scientific practices as follows:

- The scientist has to formulate empirically answerable questions about phenomena, establish what is already known, and determine what questions have yet to be satisfactorily answered.
- Scientists construct and use a wide variety of models and simulations to help develop explanations about natural phenomena.
- Scientists plan and carry out a systematic investigation, which requires the identification of what is to be recorded and, if applicable, what are to be treated as the dependent and independent variables.
- Scientists use a range of tools, including tabulation, graphical interpretation, visualisation and statistical analysis, to identify the significant features and patterns in the data.
- Mathematics and computation are used for a range of tasks, such as constructing simulations, statistically analysing data and recognising, expressing and applying quantitative relationships.
- The goal for students is to construct logically coherent explanations of phenomena that incorporate their current understanding of science, or a model that represents it, and are consistent with the available evidence.
- Scientists must defend their explanations, formulate evidence based on a solid foundation of data, examine their own understanding in light of the evidence and comments offered by others, and collaborate with peers in searching for the best explanation for the phenomenon being investigated.
- A major practice of science is the communication of ideas and the results of inquiry: orally, in writing, with the use of tables, diagrams, graphs and equations, and by engaging in extended discussions with scientific peers.

It is also evident from these aspects of science-as-practice that most of them are associated with multiple representations. Scientists communicate their findings in various forms for their peers to validate the data and establish its reliability. The use of models, textual explanations, symbolic and graphical representations all form part of multiple representations.

Osborne (2014) argued that epistemic knowledge is a necessity in science and it comprises two components: (a) Knowledge of the constructs and defining features essential to the process of knowledge-building in science, and (b) The role of these constructs in justifying the knowledge produced by science. The manner in which scientific practices are advanced is directly related to the epistemic frames adopted in the classroom. The next section outlines this construct.

Students' epistemic framing

Framing is the process of making sense of what is occurring in a particular social activity. It is useful in the teaching and learning context because students can participate while teachers create the context (Campbell & Fazio, 2018). Shaffer (2006:228) proposed that:

> Epistemic frames are a form of knowing *with* that comprise, for a particular community, knowing *where* to begin looking and asking questions, knowing *what* constitutes appropriate evidence to consider or information to assess, knowing *how* to go about gathering that evidence, and knowing *when* to draw a conclusion and/or move on to a different issue.

These epistemic frames are also associated with particular communities of practice and serve as the organising principle for practice. In the science classroom, students seldom get an opportunity to assess the evidence to make sense of a concept. This approach to knowledge building in the classroom ties in with the focus of scientific practices to develop the epistemic knowledge of the prospective science teacher. It also emphasises the importance of scaffolding as the teacher provides the prompts to allow the student to operate in the ZPD and promotes higher-order thinking.

Sin (2014) suggested that the relationship between pedagogy and how epistemology informs (or can inform) learning and teaching in Physics has been neglected. The author argued that if this was done it would harmonise "learning and teaching in physics with the nature of knowledge and the process of knowledge creation characteristic of the discipline with a view to enhancing student learning" (343). The prevalence of constructivism promotes an active engagement of the learner with the environment in order to gain conceptual understanding. At an undergraduate level there is, however, a disjuncture between the social constructivist practices of professional physicists and classroom pedagogy, which is generally informed by positivist epistemology. Scientists socially construct knowledge by engaging in research in the laboratory, whereas science is presented as facts and laws in the classroom. Students are expected to imbibe this knowledge in a systematic fashion, which contradicts the general messiness of knowledge making. It is these positivist-teaching approaches that "conceal the epistemic properties of scientific practice" (Sin, 2014:353).

Schuster et al. (2018) used two epistemic approaches to develop students' conceptual understanding of core ideas in science. In the one approach, "the core concepts and principles are presented and explained by the instructor as established science knowledge, while in the other the core ideas are co-developed by students and instructor in guided-inquiry fashion" (391). On the one hand science is presented as an established body of immutable knowledge which the teacher directs; whereas the other approach "casts learning as science-in-the-making, and aims to reflect not only what we know but how we come to know it" (Schuster, 2018:392). The point is made that the approaches do not differ because the one promotes passivity and the other active engagement; rather, both are learning-centred involving the student and teacher alike. The interesting conclusion of the study was that the two contrasting epistemic modes yielded similar learning gains for either approach.

Stroupe (2014:488) argued that: "Reframing students' learning expectations around legitimate participation in science-as-practice requires that they take on a new role as *epistemic agents*—individuals or groups who take, or are granted, responsibility for shaping the knowledge and practice of a community". The author recognised that this is challenging given that classrooms are conservative spaces where the teacher is the sole dispenser of knowledge and the student the recipient.

The above discussion provides me with a conceptual framework to analyse how pre-service teachers develop their pedagogy for science teaching. In summary, the following points emerge in relation to the analysis:

- Science students acquire their disciplinary knowledge in communities of practice. There is a disconnect between the way in which knowledge is presented as an accumulation-of-facts as opposed to the way in which scientists produce knowledge through a process of peer review.
- Sociocultural theory provides a useful lens in science education as it shows how knowledge is mediated in a social setting. Vygotsky's notion of the ZPD is particularly significant in developing students' higher-order thinking skills.
- The use of semiotic tools in multiple representations is important in the teaching and learning process as teachers use them to explain concepts while students use them to develop understanding of a concept.
- Teachers should promote science-as-practice as it exposes students to epistemic practices to develop scientific knowledge.
- It is essential to know what epistemic frame is adopted during teaching as the transmission mode encourages science-as-fact whereas a sociocultural approach supports science-in-the making.

The research questions that I frame relate to concerns that I have about how pre-service science teachers develop their pedagogy for teaching. These are:
1. What semiotic tools do pre-service science teachers use to appropriate knowledge through representational activity?
2. What epistemic approach do pre-service science teachers use to promote science-as-practice in the classroom?

3. Do pre-service science teachers scaffold concepts to promote higher-order thinking in the classroom?

In the following section, I examine vignettes of pre-service science teachers' presentation of lessons in different contexts. Each teaching and learning context is unique, but it is a social activity which I am interested in analysing in terms of how knowledge building unfolds in the shared space of the classroom. I first present an example of my own practice as an opportunity for self-reflection. Schussler et al. (2008) have argued that in teacher education, reflection before, during and after a lesson is necessary to implement new classroom teaching practices.

Reflections on my own practice

I introduce my students to a simple physics lesson that deals with the concept of refraction that is centred on the notion of a "Big Idea". This entails an observable phenomenon for which a plausible explanation must be provided (Harlen, 2010). I emphasise the macro-level observable using our senses, and the micro-level explanation, which requires a model or theory to help explain the phenomenon. I also consider this learning environment to be the creation of a science community of practice (Stroupe, 2014). The lesson is presented as a model that could be embraced by pre-service teachers when they enact their own lessons, as it demonstrates science-as-practice and the use of different semiotic tools, in addition to the verbal and non-verbal (such as gestures) explanations used.

In the lesson, I use a simulation to develop the meaning of the concept of refraction. Computer simulations can provide learning opportunities that allow students to deal with virtual phenomena and to manipulate or modify parameters that would otherwise be impossible to observe (López & Pintó, 2017). Figure 9.2 shows a screenshot of the simulation for the bending of light.

Through a series of questions to encourage students to think beyond the obvious, and to scaffold their thinking, we arrive at the definition that the light must strike obliquely, and be moving from one medium to another of different optical density, for bending (refraction) to take place. Data is then collected by tabulating the angle of incidence and refraction using a protractor. Using Snell's law we find the refractive index of glass by plotting a graph and emphasising the dependent and independent variables. I also explain that we need to interpret the gradient of the graph and find the inverse relationship. The formation of an image by the human eye and how a rainbow is formed are also discussed. These are all applications of refraction as shown in Figure 9.3.

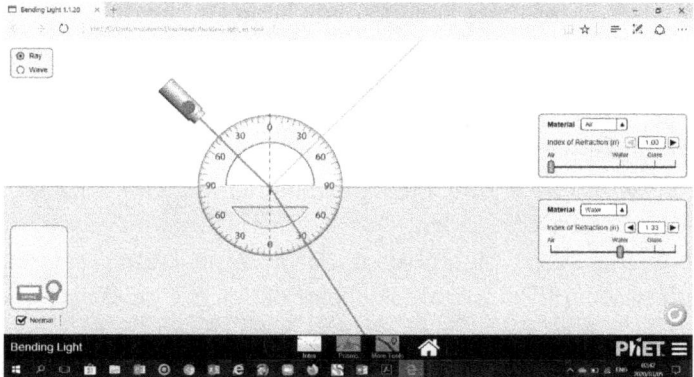

Figure 9.2 Refraction of light

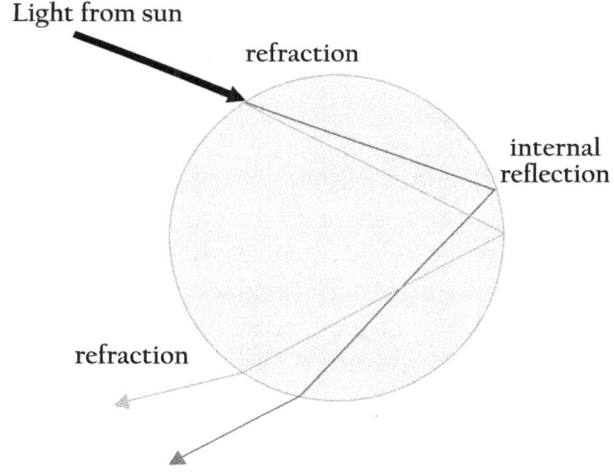

Figure 9.3 Formation of a rainbow[2]

The content requires higher-order thinking and links the concept to the everyday experiences of the student, such as how we are able to form an image of an object that we observe. In this lesson, I would argue that I have framed most of the scientific practices outlined page 151. A question is posed about the refractive index of glass, and an investigation is planned using a simulation as a model. Multiple other representations flow from this representational model. These include the tabulation of data and the plotting of a graph. The data are interpreted and analysed using mathematics and from this, explanations are constructed and communicated. According to Stroupe (2014:492), "Teachers enacting ambitious instruction, in which students learn science-as-practice,

2 https://bit.ly/3kMRVfv

help reframe students' roles from knowledge recipients to *epistemic agents*". I would therefore offer this lesson as a model to enact in the classroom as it embodies most of the elements of science-as-practice.

It is from the perspective of the cauldron of classroom practice that I now turn to analyse my own students' epistemic approaches. I present a multi-case study of five PGCE students presenting either a microteaching lesson to a group of learners at the university, or a lesson during teaching practice at a secondary school. All five are Bachelor of Science graduates and majored in Chemistry. The students consented to have their lessons video-recorded as part of a project that focuses on pedagogy in the science classroom. Each lesson plan was presented to me as a word document and feedback was provided immediately after the lesson concluded. The lessons and contexts in which they unfold are described and analysed in terms of the framework offered above.

Student 1

The student chose to teach the concept of magnetism to a Grade 10 Physical Sciences class. This is a microteaching lesson for learners from a middle class girls' school where there are ample resources to teach the subject as well as a permanent laboratory assistant who prepares experiments for the science classes. The school also has an impeccable record in the National Senior Certificate (NSC) examination having achieved a 100% pass rate for a number of years, and being ranked in the top 10 schools in the Western Cape province, South Africa.

The epistemic approach used by the student is largely teacher-centred with the idea of a magnetic force being foregrounded in the lesson. The transmission mode of teaching dominates, with science content presented as established fact although some of the ideas are practically demonstrated and represented diagrammatically. The core ideas are referenced to the textbook, which represents an accumulation of science facts or canonical knowledge. Student 1 exemplifies this as follows:

> I think in the textbook they write it like this.
>
> What is magnetism ... what do you think it is? I have two definitions here.
>
> You will see the ends of the magnet have...

This could be labelled a conservative approach where learning takes place through rote learning and memorisation of facts. The teacher retains cognitive authority and the learners are not engaged in science-as-practice. When questions are posed and the learners respond, there is then a mere confirmation of their answers as either right or wrong. There is no engagement to elaborate and discuss the answers. Thus there is no shift in cognitive authority so that the learners become epistemic agents. It is evident from the analysis of the lesson that limited effort was made to represent the concept of magnetic force through different semiotic tools. The notion of science-in-the-making from a sociocultural perspective was absent, and there was no scaffolding of the concepts to promote higher-order thinking.

There were no restrictions placed on the pre-service science teachers in terms of the approach they could use to teach a particular topic, especially if it was taught at the university to a group of learners during microteaching. An opportunity to present science-as-practice was therefore lost with a group of learners well suited to such an approach.

Student 2

A microteaching chemistry lesson is presented to a group of learners from a high school where the languages of teaching are Afrikaans and English. The pre-service science teacher presents this particular lesson in Afrikaans. The school also has well-established science laboratories having recently refurbished them.

The lesson focuses on the core idea of a chemical or physical change. At the start of the lesson, the group of learners are called to the demonstration table to observe a certain reaction. The pre-service science teacher had prepared the same sample the day before in the event of something going wrong. She asks the learners to observe and predict whether a physical or chemical change will take place. As the reaction proceeds, she appears a little impatient and states the following:

> You have to wait a little and then you will see a colour change. This is normally an indication of a chemical change.

Having asked the learners to state what they think the reaction is, she then gives the answer herself. This is a clear indication of her retaining cognitive authority by giving the correct answer even before the learners respond. There is no room for alternative answers, or an opportunity to speculate and discuss events as they unfold in reality.

Later on, the learners engage in a hands-on activity using material to represent a model of a chemical reaction such as the formation of water. This is clearly science-as-practice in action because models are used to explain a certain phenomenon. However, the moment the model deviates from the correct scientific representation the student teacher offers the correct answer.

This turned out to be an interesting lesson in that elements of science-as-fact and science-in-the-making are present. The pre-service science teacher resorts to ultimately retaining cognitive authority, and fails to allow mutual knowledge building in the classroom for the learners to develop their role as epistemic agents. There is an attempt to use different representations, but scaffolding to allow deep learning was somehow negated when the student teacher intervened by providing the answers when there was potential to engage the learners in discussion.

Student 3

A chemistry lesson, which focused on chemical bonding, is presented during microteaching at the university. The learners are from a poorly resourced school and science has not been one of the school's strong subjects as evidenced by the NSC results. The number of learners doing science has remained low over the years, despite the support that the university's Chemistry department provides to promote science at the school.

The pre-service science teacher starts with a question: Where have you come across chemical bonding? In your books?

> Learner: In Life Orientation.
>
> Student teacher: So is it to bond your family members? Okay, nice one.

After this opening, the lesson is presented with a statement of the science facts and no engagement of science ideas with the learners. Formal definitions are provided so that the notion of science-as-fact dominates. Cognitive authority resides with the student teacher, and as a result, the learners do not become epistemic agents. This vision of science is a conservative approach to teaching and does not promote science-as-practice. Learners' ideas are not supported to come to the fore through engagement in discussion, or using models to explain phenomena. This particular class exemplifies one where teacher-talk dominates and the building of a community of practice is absent. There is also no attempt to promote the use of multiple representations, or to scaffold any concepts to stimulate higher-order engagement with the concepts.

Student 4

The student presents the topic of mechanical energy to a Grade 10 class at a dual medium school in a small town during teaching practice. Both English and Afrikaans are used during the lesson. The school is reasonably resourced with access to some laboratory and audio-visual equipment.

The student opens the lesson by asking if anyone can provide a definition of mechanical energy. A learner responds with a good answer, which the student teacher confirms as correct. The lesson proceeds with constant questions being asked of the learners. Derivation of units is done to confirm that energy is measured in Joules. A pendulum is then demonstrated to explain conservation of mechanical energy. Graphs are drawn to further illustrate the point. The learners are then given a few questions to solve where they apply the law of conservation of mechanical energy.

This is also an interesting lesson to analyse as both science-as-fact and science-as-practice are present. When learners answer the questions, the core science facts are merely stated and confirmed by the student teacher. The use of the pendulum to explain the concept of conservation of mechanical energy provides evidence that the student teacher attempted to engage in different representational activities.

The fact that the student teacher ensures that all the answers are scientifically correct with no room for discussion means that cognitive authority still resides with her. There was also no attempt made to promote higher-order thinking by scaffolding the concepts. In fact, the lesson seemed to be well rehearsed with a reluctance to deviate from the script. This is another opportunity missed for learners to develop epistemic knowledge. They could have been engaged in meaningful argument, a feature of scientific practice.

Student 5

The student taught chemical solutions to a Grade 11 science class at a township school during teaching practice. The school is poorly resourced, but promotes science teaching and learning through active participation in support programmes provided by the university.

The student sets up a data projector, which he connected to a laptop computer. He proceeds to present the core concepts of the lesson using PowerPoint. Some of the key concepts are explained using a simulation. The learners then complete some problem-solving exercises. Statement of the science facts dominate the lesson, and the student teacher makes no effort to promote higher-order thinking.

While some elements of science-as-practice are present – such as using a model to explain a phenomenon – the student teacher largely retains cognitive authority. No attempt is made to do any science investigation, or to discuss and construct explanations. The learners are minimally exposed to use of different representational forms during the lesson. What was striking, and is something I have noticed on a few occasions, is that the learners would in unison state the definition of terms out loudly. English is not their mother tongue and the teacher would often code-switch to the local language of isiXhosa in an attempt to clarify the terms used in the lesson.

Conclusion

The pedagogy that unfolded in these five cases largely mirrors what happens in many South African classrooms. Stroupe (2014:488) referred to American classrooms when he stated: "Conservative science teaching prevents opportunities for students to become epistemic agents by promoting the completion of curricular activities rather than sense-making". One could substitute 'American' with South African here and the statement would still be appropriate. Teachers are under great pressure to complete an overloaded curriculum, and hence, often resort to presenting "science-as-accumulated-knowledge" (Stroupe, 2014: 490). Whether or not they are skilled enough to shift beyond the epistemic boundaries that deliver the canons of the textbook, and expect students to deliver likewise, is a moot point (Stroupe, Caballero & White, 2018). Pre-service science teachers, from the evidence presented in their lessons, appear to be no different. Despite having more freedom to explore beyond these limitations, to a large degree they resort to enacting the curriculum through conservative teaching and fail to make inroads to become epistemic agents that advance science-as-practice in the classroom.

Reform efforts in teacher education in South Africa must focus on the establishment of a new cohort of qualified teachers who meet the standards of the *Minimum Requirements for Teacher Education Qualifications* (DHET, 2015). The policy advocates "incorporating situational and contextual elements that assist teachers in developing competences that enable them to deal with diversity and transformation" (9). Science teacher education is uniquely positioned to contribute to producing teachers who are able to adapt to a changing environment in which technology plays an increasingly significant role in teaching and learning. A sociocultural perspective addresses the interactions that the teacher and learner should have to use the tools of the practice to explicitly mediate scientific knowledge, and bring about transformation by building a community of practice.

In this chapter, I have proposed that multiple representations are pervasive in all of their facets – verbal, textual, graphical or symbolic – as such, allowing enculturation into the science learning community. For this reason, pre-service teachers should be encouraged to use them in the classroom. However, the analysis of the lessons shows that student teachers fall short in the way they use multiple representations during a lesson. Multiple representations are also a powerful way to scaffold the learning of a concept and operate in the ZPD of the learner. Again, the pre-service teachers fail in building knowledge through science-as-practice in the classroom and developing the epistemic agency of the learners.

These findings show that some student teachers have an epistemic approach that promotes science as an accumulation of knowledge or as an established body of knowledge. Others tentatively engage in scientific practices that promote the acquisition of epistemic knowledge, but at the same time they have a conservative teaching approach that holds onto cognitive authority within the classroom. Shifting of epistemic agency, which ideally should be happening, is all too often absent.

There are many reasons for the lack of this shift towards epistemic agency. One is the fact that students feel constrained by the curriculum and only teach what is prescribed. Another is that they come from a discipline that places an emphasis on the correctness of scientific facts; therefore, they only provide learners with textbook-driven answers. It would take more than just showing them how it could be done, but perhaps our assessment methods should explicitly focus on the extent to which scientific practices are adopted in the classroom.

As a science teacher educator, I have to acknowledge that doing work that disrupts the thinking of the pre-service science teacher is difficult, especially if it goes against years of doing science where the teacher retained cognitive authority. If the expectation is that the pre-service teacher must make a shift and appropriate epistemic agency, and in turn foster the same in their classrooms, then there has to be a fundamental change in the way we teach and learn science. We want to make science more meaningful so that the learner sees the value of the discipline in everyday life, but we continue to treat learners as passive recipients of knowledge. This tension is unlikely to go away so we must take small steps to bring about a change in mindset in our pre-service science teachers who are the teachers of tomorrow.

Acknowledgement

The financial assistance of the National Research Foundation (NRF) towards this research is hereby acknowledged. Opinions expressed and conclusions arrived at, are those of the author and are not necessarily to be attributed to the NRF.

References

Ainsworth, S. 2008. The educational value of multiple-representations when learning complex scientific concepts. In: J.K. Gilbert, M. Reiner & M. Nakhleh (eds), *Visualisation: Theory and practice in science education*. Dordrecht: Springe, pp. 191-208. https://doi.org/10.1007/978-1-4020-5267-5_9

Campbell, T. & Fazio, X. 2018. Epistemic frames as an analytical framework for understanding the representation of scientific activity in a modeling-based learning unit. *Research in Science Education*, 1-22.

Daniels, H. 2001. *Vygotsky and pedagogy*. London: Routledge Falmer. https://doi.org/10.4324/9780203469576

DHET (Department of Higher Education and Training). 2015. *Revised policy on the minimum requirements for teacher education qualifications*. Government Gazette No 38487. Pretoria, South Africa: Department of Higher Education and Training.

Erduran, S. & Dagher, Z. (eds). 2014. *Reconceptualizing the nature of science for science education: Scientific knowledge, practices and other family categories*. Dordrecht: Springer.

Haefner, L. & Zembal-Saul, C. 2004. Learning by doing? Prospective elementary teachers' developing understandings of scientific inquiry and science teaching and learning. *International Journal of Science Education*, 26(13):1653-1674. https://doi.org/10.1080/0950069042000230709

Harlen, W. 2010. *Principles and big ideas in science education*. Available at: https://bit.ly/3kEbmXS [accessed 6 February 2020].

Hordern, J. 2015. Teaching, teacher formation, and specialised professional practice. *European Journal of Teacher Education*, 38(4):431-444. https://doi.org/10.1080/02619768.2015.1056910

John-Steiner, V. & Mahn, H.1996. Sociocultural approaches to learning and development: A Vygotskian framework. *Educational psychologist*, 31(3-4):191-206. https://doi.org/10.1080/00461520.1996.9653266

Kozma, R. & Russell, J. 2005. Students becoming chemists: Developing representational competence. In: J.K. Gilbert (ed.), *Visualizations in science education*. Dordrecht: Springer, pp. 121-146. https://doi.org/10.1007/1-4020-3613-2_8

Leach, J. & Scott, P. 2003. Individual and sociocultural views of learning in science education. *Science & Education*, 12(1):91-113. https://doi.org/10.1023/A:1022665519862

Liang, L.L. & Richardson, G.M. 2009. Enhancing prospective teachers' science teaching efficacy beliefs through scaffolded, student-directed inquiry. *Journal of Elementary Science Education*, 21(1):51-66. https://doi.org/10.1007/BF03174715

López, V. & Pintó, R. 2017. Computer simulations and students' difficulties in reading visual representations in science education. In: M. Pietrocola & I. Gurgel (eds), *Crossing the border of the traditional science curriculum*. Rotterdam: Sense Publishers, pp. 95-114. https://doi.org/10.1007/978-94-6351-041-7_6

Moore, T.J., Guzey, S.S., Roehrig, G.H. & Lesh, R.A. 2018. Representational fluency: A means for students to develop STEM literacy. In: K.L. Daniel (ed.), *Towards a framework for representational competence in science education*. Cham: Springer, pp. 13-30. https://doi.org/10.1007/978-3-319-89945-9_2

National Research Council. 1996. *National science education standards*. Washington, D.C: National Academy Press.

National Research Council. 2012. *A framework for K–12 science education: Practices, crosscutting concepts, and core ideas*. Washington, DC: The National Academies Press.

Osborne, J. 2014. Teaching scientific practices: Meeting the challenge of change. *Journal of Science Teacher Education*, 25(2):177-196. https://doi.org/10.1007/s10972-014-9384-1

Prain, V. & Waldrip, B. 2006. An exploratory study of teachers' and students' use of multi-modal representations of concepts in primary science. *International Journal of Science Education*, 28(15):1843-1866. https://doi.org/10.1080/09500690600718294

Rau, M.A. 2017. Conditions for the effectiveness of multiple visual representations in enhancing STEM learning. *Educational Psychology Review*, 29(4):717-761. https://doi.org/10.1007/s10648-016-9365-3

Rau, M.A. 2020. Cognitive and socio-cultural theories on competencies and practices involved in learning with multiple external representations. In: P. Van Meter, A. List, D. Lombardi & P. Kendeou (eds), Handbook of learning from multiple representations and perspectives. New York: Routledge, pp. 17-32. https://doi.org/10.4324/9780429443961-3

Schussler, E., Torres, L.E., Rybczynski, S., Gerald, G.W., Monroe, E., Sarkar, P., Shahi, D. & Osman, M.A. 2008. Transforming the teaching of science graduate students through reflection. *Journal of College Science Teaching*, 38(1):32-36.

Schuster, D., Cobern, W.W., Adams, B.A., Undreiu, A. & Pleasants, B. 2018. Learning of core disciplinary ideas: Efficacy comparison of two contrasting modes of science instruction. *Research in Science Education*, 48(2):389-435. https://doi.org/10.1007/s11165-016-9573-3

Scott, S. & Palincsar, A. 2013. Sociocultural theory. Available at: https://bit.ly/2IGus2M [accessed 6 April 2020].

Shaffer, D.W. 2006. Epistemic frames for epistemic games. *Computers & education*, 46(3):223-234. https://doi.org/10.1016/j.compedu.2005.11.003

Sin, C. 2014. Epistemology, sociology, and learning and teaching in physics. *Science Education*, 98(2):342-365. https://doi.org/10.1002/sce.21100

Stroupe, D. 2014. Examining classroom science practice communities: How teachers and students negotiate epistemic agency and learn science-as-practice. *Science Education*, 98(3):487-516. https://doi.org/10.1002/sce.21112

Stroupe, D., Caballero, M.D. & White, P. 2018. Fostering students' epistemic agency through the co-configuration of moth research. *Science Education*, 102(6):1176-1200. https://doi.org/10.1002/sce.21469

Tang, K.S., Degado, C. & Moje, E. 2014. An integrative framework for the analysis of multiple and multimodal representations for meaning-making in science education. *Science Education*, 98:305-326. https://doi.org/10.1002/sce.21099

Van der Veer, R. 2007. Vygotsky in Context: 1900–1935. In: H. Daniels, M. Cole & J. Wertsch (eds), *The Cambridge companion to Vygotsky*. New York: Cambridge University Press, pp. 21-49. https://doi.org/10.1017/CCOL0521831040.002

Vygotsky, L.S. 1978. *Mind in society*. Cambridge, MA: Harvard University Press.

Waldrip, B. & Prain, V. 2012. *Learning from and through representations in science. In: Second international handbook of science education*. Dordrecht: Springer, pp. 145-155. https://doi.org/10.1007/978-1-4020-9041-7_12

Wertsch J. 2007. Mediation. In: H. Daniels, M. Cole & J. Wertsch (eds), *The Cambridge companion to Vygotsky*. Cambridge: Cambridge University Press, pp. 178-192. https://doi.org/10.1017/CCOL0521831040.008

Won, M., Yoon, H. & Treagust, D.F. 2014. Students' learning strategies with multiple representations: Explanations of the human breathing mechanism. *Science Education*, 98(5):840-866. https://doi.org/10.1002/sce.21128

SECTION C
Conclusion

An agenda for reinventing teacher education in South Africa: Next steps for deliberation

Marie Brennan

Reflecting with and for teacher education

Looking into South African teacher education from the outside, it feels very familiar. How can this be, when I am from Australia, a 'global North' country in the geographic South? Our demographic and economic conditions are quite different. There are fewer than 3% of the Indigenous peoples of Australia left alive compared to the 75–80% in South Africa. Australia, while still working through colonial legacies, did not experience an apartheid regime. Yet there are common historical trajectories. Our countries are both former colonies of the British Empire, the logic of mass schooling and its associated inequalities are palpable, and teacher education is positioned to service the formation of the nation state through providing teachers who accept their role. South Africa suffered its emergence into the post-apartheid period in the heyday of economic globalisation – which also altered what might be expected of the nation state in its relations with citizens, including through education. Despite this, as I have learned, most people invested hope for shifting opportunities for the majority black population, and other minority groups, in education. Yet, as can more clearly be seen now, education cannot shift societal mores, habits and identities without major public shifts in other domains, including economic redistribution and opportunities to participate in debates and reinventions of institutions. Education can be part of such important shifts but cannot do so 'on behalf of' everyone else, every other institution.

The Organisation for Economic Co-operation and Development (OECD), emphasising its economic credentials, has published a number of reports giving priority to the role of schools, teachers and teacher education in building national economic competitiveness. This has tended, in many countries, to place economic purposes at the centre of the educational effort, with significant push-back among the profession in many countries over some time (Furlong, Cochran-Smith & Brennan, 2009). This reminder goes some way to explain why we in Australia have similar debates as those represented in this book. How do schooling and its teachers deal with diversity and inequality, social stratification and the hopes invested in education to provide social and economic mobility? How do students and communities deal with the differences between those who teach and their students? How do beginning teachers learn to work with students different to themselves – culturally, linguistically, economically? In secondary schools, how does the subject knowledge of schools and teacher qualifications in disciplines begin to recognise other knowledges? And, we also raise the question of mediating between traditional 'ownership' of their units/modules by individual academics and the need to create a programme that builds on its parts.

We have in common the regulatory nation state and the bureaucracy that is inter-nationally prevalent to surveille education institutions, establish standards via standardisation, approve programmes and curriculum, and measure performance in teaching and research. Yet the conditions in our two countries are quite different, though we share many of the effects in our work and workload. In recent years, teacher educators in many countries have been constrained into a compliance register: worried about performativity measures and regulations. Moving beyond compliance (Cochran-Smith et al., 2018) into a broader, more collaborative set of research programmes is critical to support one another and our own university students, as well as the schools and communities they serve. This book brings out ways in which the regulatory state works its way into one university programme. Examining it as a whole is quite instructive about conditions in South Africa, the 'practice architectures' (Kemmis, 2009) which pull together the 'sayings, doings and relatings' which are taken for granted in the everyday work of the faculty.

Issues set up in this book

As the Introduction lays out, the chapters here arise from shared discussions across staff in the whole Postgraduate Certificate in Education (PGCE) programme. This in itself is an achievement. There are few large-scale studies of teacher education, and most who research in teacher education usually do so in small single classroom studies, remaining in disciplinary silos: science education, education psychology, teaching art or sociology, for example. We write on professional placement, on the pedagogies of our own subject. The lack of larger studies is partly an issue of poor funding, partly a workload issue, and points to a lack of respect for practitioner-oriented research domains. When even the USA with all its resources, has to commission research agendas for teacher education (Cochran-Smith & Zeichner, 2006), it is not surprising that poorer countries do not have vibrant research cultures in teacher education. Ken Zeichner's (2007) call to accumulate studies across what have been largely individual self-studies thus has global resonance for teacher educators. He reminds us all that we have to consider the theoretical project as well as work towards improvement of practice.

The teacher educators here have taken the important step of problematising the programmatic issues underpinning each of their subjects by engaging in shared deliberation on key starting points. These include:

- "How to navigate within teacher education from the ravages of apartheid education to inclusive, democratic practices that address the developmental needs of the majority of our citizens.
- The desire to move out of academic 'silos' and to work across subjects and departments to build a shared understanding of the programme.
- How to ensure structural and conceptual coherence across the programme, while allowing lecturers the academic freedom to engage students critically within their discipline.
- How to engage with the demands of knowledge-building in the twenty-first century.
- How to integrate different forms of knowledge across the curriculum". (America, Edwards & Robinson, Chapter 1).

The book represents a set of engagements with these questions, and in the process establishes a longer term set of issues to grapple with, as the programme design evolves in practice and in relation to policy guidelines. Such shared deliberation among programme staff contributes to the possibility of iterative cycles contributing to knowledge-in-practice and knowledge-of-practice. In a sense, the questions open up what Freire (1993/1970) called generative themes – problematising key dimensions of teacher education practice as the programme, its staff and university transition to a changing world. The COVID-19 pandemic adds further fuel to questions about the purposes of schooling, the role of the teacher, the practices of pedagogies and the potential contribution which teacher education might make to the schooling sector and the wider South African society.

What do I see as being put on the teacher education scholarly-praxis agenda in the book? These questions above open up serious work, both specific to South Africa and also relevant in other countries and regions. The address made to them emerges from representing that work, allowing the authors the space to examine such issues as:

- Who are our pre-service teachers?
- What do they need to know and be able to do?
- How do students and academic staff relate among themselves and learn with and from one another?
- What are our curriculum design and pedagogic practices?
- How are they shaped by the particular university in which we work?
- How do we change our practices?
- What do each of our modules offer towards a programme?
- What key concepts are being offered for exploration and understanding?
- What is a good teacher? A good pre-service teacher? A good teacher educator?
- What conceptual resources and language are needed for pre-service teachers to understand and teach for multilingual, diverse cultures?
- How do we contribute to changing schooling?
- How do we meet changes in the society more broadly, to contribute to social justice?

In taking up these starter questions outlined in the introductory chapter as the basis for discussion, I would suggest that we are invited to follow them up as a way of problematising university pedagogy and partnership with schools in the decolonial moment (Soudien, 2020). In South Africa, this follows the #FeesMustFall and 'decolonise the curriculum' movements, which teacher educators have joined, although they have seldom articulated issues specific to their field of knowledge and practice. These are programme design questions which put a spotlight on individual academic pedagogic practices but also imply questions about what is possible to do differently across individual modules.

What is post-apartheid teacher education in a teacher education programme?

In the introduction, the editors noted the first question of how teacher education deals with "the ravages of apartheid": post-apartheid teacher education is challenged to unpack the deeply historically formed practices of both the university and schooling. These chapters show some key dimensions of how the challenges work themselves into the daily practices of academic teaching, of curriculum design, relations among pre-service teachers and between teachers and pre-service teachers. Post-apartheid is represented in a range of ways in these chapters. In some chapters it is contextual: a societal condition, historically formed, which schooling is aiming to address and thus teacher education must focus on building greater social justice through teaching. Other chapters assume this context without naming it, while referring more to diversity, identity and/or interdependence as ways to enter into understanding learners. For two chapters, post-apartheid is *embodied* in the PGCE programme through reflection on one's own formation and its implications for teaching: Joorst (Chapter 5) as a teacher educator embodying the racialised 'other' relating to largely white students through his pedagogies; and Fataar and Feldman's (Chapter 6) exemplars of student reflective writing assignments which name and contest ongoing racialised inequalities in daily life, including at the university itself.

The inequalities in even a basic level of schooling provision in South Africa are continually 'present' in the different chapters' efforts to understand difference and diversity. The most common way of addressing this challenge is taken up through the exploration of ethics:

- the ethics of pre-service teachers' 'agency' in teacher practice (Robinson),
- understanding healthy human development as social and inter-dependent – who our learners are and how we support their quest to become more human (Conradie),
- teaching pre-service teachers to undertake ethical reflection of self-formation in relation to historical, racialised institutions (Fataar & Feldman),
- integrating ethics into business studies as a way to problematise business practices for citizens (America),
- emphasising the importance of selecting curriculum knowledge of worth for the future (Botha), and
- the question of what sciences might contribute to a more just society (Edwards).

These ethical questions are much more than 'professional ethics'. They insist on citizens, including student teachers, being able to explore ethics in practice as part of contributing to their society. The ethical responsibilities of teacher educators in developing those capacities themselves, through reflection and critique of their own practices, underpins each chapter. In making that effort public, bravely, the authors make it possible to engage in conversation to develop new practices for the university and in relation to teachers and schools.

Having made their reflections and curriculum work public, these teacher educators have opened up new questions, which need to be addressed together. Unpacking the systemic and structural in teacher education's daily practices (see Kemmis et al., 2017) requires further dialogue and expanded reflection. What is the next move for this faculty and its programme? In what follows, I take up the absent presences and the issues laid on the table to invite further exploration, particularly as they resonate with me as regular visiting scholar and as co-practitioner across the Indian Ocean.

(Post) apartheid

'Apartheid' and post-apartheid are rarely mentioned in the chapters. Rather they appear as both ever-present and assumed within the university and the schooling system. Does (post) apartheid need to be unpacked more explicitly in public? Or are the terms 'social justice' and 'diversity' enough to understand and develop emerging practices? Not being based in South Africa, I don't know. However, I would suggest that in the next phase of academic deliberation and sharing, it would be worth using these chapters to surface assumptions about the specifics of how a programme can grapple with 'post-apartheid'. Is there a shared view? The context is quite different now than in 1994, both for school teachers and universities. Does the positioning of the staff themselves make such conversations difficult? Is the tension across practices in different modules and disciplinary traditions helpful for helping pre-service teachers to achieve a more explicit understanding of teaching and education institutions? What could an Afrikaans-background university do differently in terms of knowledge selection and university pedagogies for its diverse students? How does that desired and (im)possible condition of post-apartheid make itself visible in the pedagogical practices and embodied presence of a teacher education programme? What is at stake for the diversely disciplined and diversely backgrounded academic staff? How does post-apartheid challenge how teacher education understands its formation and disciplinary heritage? What responsibility do teacher educators have in explicit theorising on decolonising and decoloniality? Beyond a 'mission statement' or 'values statement' for a programme, how does struggling with decoloniality enter into our daily teaching practice?

In trying to unpack our work practices and identities in a colonised society, with the heavy burden of apartheid in the case of South Africa, amidst the multiple intertwined crises of capitalism, environment and the racialised, patriarchal nation state (Brennan, 2017), it is worth remembering that teacher education does carry forward all those contemporary and historical habits. They are inscribed in our own histories and careers, the institutions in which we are embedded and their artefacts, in our curriculum and pedagogies. Mostly we act both *within and against the grain*. The opportunity of reaccreditation of a programme has helped bring out what is at stake in the design and enaction of a programme, helping to question the very 'grain' itself. Every element of the 'grain' or 'grammar' of education institutions (Tyack & Tobin, 1994) has been infused with apartheid and colonial segregation legacies. It follows that the artefacts, the lecture theatres, statues and offices shape what is possible to do and imagine for teacher education curriculum and pedagogies. The knowledge-work – the content options and languages made available – have similar heritages, embedded in academic careers and qualifications, too, and academic identities. 'Reflection' is thus a heavily-laden term, one that calls for dialogue so that it is not accomplished in private but as part of the public shared work of a programme team.

South Africanising 'Productive Pedagogies'?

In grappling with the questions and starting points of their conversation, the second resource to open up dialogue among the academic faculty of the programme was that of the Productive Pedagogies. These are very familiar to me as the work derives from longitudinal study in Australian schools (Hayes, Mills, Christie & Lingard, 2006). Productive Pedagogies emphasises four dimensions of pedagogies, viz., intellectual quality, connectedness, a supportive classroom environment and working with and valuing difference. These specify pedagogical teaching and learning assemblages which produce greater access to the 'goods' of schooling for marginalised groups. Several of the chapters engaged with elements of these pedagogies, including the issue of substantive conversations necessary for intellectual quality; the significance of increasing diversity among the academic staff and the pre-service teaching body at Stellenbosch; how to build supportive learning environments based around understanding students; connectedness with the complexity of schools; and, the problem of professional placements.

Following up the Productive Pedagogies more explicitly within South African teacher education – exploring, analysing and developing pedagogies which build greater distribution of education for citizenship, participation and recognition – would be a major contribution to teacher education scholarship. It would have ramifications that challenge those university's pedagogies-as-usual that translate legacies of coloniality (Mignolo & Walsh, 2018) which further seep into, and are too little problematised in schools.

Many of the modules have taken up the Productive Pedagogies challenge. In a number of chapters, the question of intellectual quality is foregrounded. Carina America (Chapter 7) raises questions about how to address business ethics in teacher education through substantive, intellectually rich and rigorous conversations, and how this focus might address a different orientation to business and business studies for future citizens. Marie Louise Botha (Chapter 4) problematises the selection of knowledge in Curriculum Studies, asking how growth of pre-service teachers' knowledge of education might itself contribute to new futures. Building epistemological dispositions through considering key concepts in education psychology is the challenge put forward by Karlien Conradie (Chapter 3), and Nazeem Edwards (Chapter 8) wants the science educators to be able to recontextualise science knowledges for greater student engagement.

Connectedness is considered in almost every chapter. Identities are relational; relationships – e.g. Jerome Joorst's troubling of the possibilities of respectful knowing between teacher educator and pre-service teacher – are central to teaching practice. Can a pre-service teacher get to know his world? The world of township students? Conradie's argument for relational interdependence as central to building good learning does require engagement with the big issues as experienced by those we teach. Health and economic issues associated with the current global pandemic – and the maldistribution of resources to deal with it – bring out the need for ensuring that pre-service teachers and teacher educators as citizens can not only understand their world but also are in a position to build agency to address issues as they are lived, as Maureen Robinson raises in relation to professional placements. 'Relevance' depends on knowledge and grows through action across relationships.

Valuing difference, the third productive pedagogy, remains a key focus for all chapters. Fataar and Feldman (Chapter 6) argue that learning to 'become' a teacher requires attention to students' own biographic histories and trajectories so that they will be able to treat these in relation to the biographies and trajectories of students and other teachers who may be quite different from themselves. Boaventura De Sousa Santos (2018) calls such work the refusal of the 'epistemicide' of colonialism, i.e. exclusion of knowledges other than the dominant Eurocentric; the work includes their retrieval and placement back into curriculum alongside other knowledges.

The strangest aspect of teacher education at Stellenbosch University for me has been the lecture-based format for the core modules, with tutorials for these classes largely optional. Thus, 'discussion' in the compulsory modules means addressing issues in a large class (in the case of the PGCE, often more than 200 students) in a tiered lecture theatre. I find it difficult to imagine how the strong identity-shaping work of engaging and valuing difference or taking up lived issues in schools (which will be different to their own for the majority of students) can be underpinned without scheduled small tutorials for all groups. In such settings learning with and from each other can support work *against the grain*, with the emotional and intellectual embodiment required. The supportive classroom environment of Productive Pedagogies is thus a major challenge in which to build pedagogical practices in teacher education at the university and in partnership with school placements. Being electives, the subject-specific module groups are much smaller and there is more scope for social engagement; however, those teacher educators who are responsible for the core modules still try for substantive conversations in the lecture theatre; they try to make issues 'live' for pre-service teachers. Much of their creative pedagogical work lies in designing activities and assessments that support identity work and understanding of societal issues present in education institutions, as the chapters by Fataar and Feldman, Joorst and Edwards illustrate.

For me, from a settler-society where the colonial legacies of violence, patriarchy and 'epistemicide' continue to shape education institutions, the following questions arise when engaging with the Productive Pedagogies as a teacher educator:

- Is it possible to specify which pedagogies are 'productive' in teacher education classrooms in the very different and diverse nations of Australia/South Africa?
- How might pre-service teachers help to develop and document school pedagogic practices which produce greater access in Australia/South Africa?
- In what ways and around which concepts do pre-service teachers engage with intellectual quality in their study and practice of schooling and teaching?
- How does a teacher educator generate substantive conversations around key concepts pre-service teachers need to analyse and explain teaching, learning and schooling in South Africa at the current moment?
- How can university-based teacher education programme academics connect pre-service teachers with the social, political and economic issues that have and continue to shape their lives and the place of humans on the planet to inform the work of teaching?
- In building 'citizen-educators', how do teachers and teacher educators share that work with other citizens?

- How can teacher educators retrieve and/or draw on knowledges and languages which have been 'invisibilised' from inclusion in university and school curricula?
- What might be the alliances with other countries that help other decolonialising practices for teacher education to emerge?
- What pedagogic strategies support teacher educators' connection with pre-service teachers, and among the student cohort, to build assets from their own diversities that underpin the dismantling of deficit pedagogy in schools and universities?
- In what ways might township and other marginalised communities and their agencies inform and shape teacher education programmes for the majority?

Such questions, and more, could form the basis of the next stage of debate, building shared research agendas in teacher education at Stellenbosch University. In teacher education we are supposed to 'know'. We are, however, only too well aware of what we don't know. Our task is to refuse the singular, reductionist recipe approach to knowledge and to build up knowledge for and from practice. Back in 1993, Wagner argued that research programmes have both blind spots and blank spots. A blank spot represents an area that is inadequately developed within an existing matrix of phenomena for investigation and key themes and conceptual foci for a discipline. For example, we may have learned a great deal about school access in urban areas but not have much study of whether access problems are similar or different in rural and remote areas. That blank spot on the research agenda matrix can be filled in, following similar methodologies, questions and issues, and may in turn add further dimensions to the original studies and their questions and findings. Blind spots, on the other hand, are those which our current methodologies and foci do not reveal, questions we have not asked nor even thought need to be asked.

The post-apartheid South Africa has necessarily forced teacher educators to address a number of blank spots and blind spots. Social, economic and political shifts have a history of doing that. Establishing an evolving research agenda through shared exploration of the design and conduct of a teacher education programme has rarely been achieved, particularly in countries where capitalist redistribution does not thrive. The 'matrix' of teacher education research has to move beyond a kind of universalist definition of current assumptions of the phenomena to be studied and the resources for studying them. The Covid-19 global pandemic is similarly raising issues into awareness so that new questions can be asked – not just of the political, economic and health systems, but also of teacher education. There are multiple ways in which blind spots can be surfaced, although there are often gatekeepers who make it difficult to ask new questions.

A key way to bring blind spots to the surface is to borrow issues from other disciplines. Wagner terms this: "one discipline's row, another's column" in the research agenda matrix (1993:18). Zeichner (2007) understands that building knowledge across such studies opens up new questions for knowledge-in-practice, making possible new research agendas. By working from a group of studies, such as those represented in this book, it is possible that the book can become more than the sum of its parts, as single self-study cases. Represented in this book, and possibly more in its underpinning programme dialogic deliberations, are a diverse set of research methods and disciplinary orientations that can challenge one another's blind spots – and in the process put new issues and practices for further research in teacher education. It may well be that a social psychologist's orientation to identity can open up questions of social inter-dependence that allow new questions of the historian or the sociologist of education. 'Racialisation' processes are differently understood by literacy educators or environment and health educators. How do they come together to develop more inclusive research agendas for teacher education? It may be useful to examine debates in other former colonies' societies to help bring out an explicit articulation of issues within a South African context such as among Canadian First Nations (Amsler, Kerr & Andreotti, 2020; Dénommé-Welch & Montero, 2014) or Maori experience in New Zealand (Smith & Smith, 2019), unpacking the materiality of practices in Tuck and Wang's approach to decoloniality as "more than a metaphor" (2012:1).

The question facing the reader and the Faculty of Education at Stellenbosch University, now, is not so much 'What can I learn from this book?' – although there is much provoked by the different chapters – but more a question of: What can the authors teach us next? Yes, the teacher educators here have to do more work, as do we all. Taking up this challenge means engaging in further investigations, opening up one's own identity and its historical trajectory to colleagues to enable a shared problematisation about both education and teacher education's positioning in South Africa. That requires building a level of trust and knowledge of one another that is difficult to achieve. However, there is some dialogic history to build on, and further interrogate, together. Covid-19 adds even more urgency to this demand to open ourselves up to rethinking teacher education, teaching and learning, and schooling more generally. Future questions that arise from thinking of next steps across these chapters will deepen the conversations and deliberations among programme staff, inviting others – including myself – to pursue them further. Teacher education scholarship will be enriched, along with its practice. The next book should be even more brave.

References

Amsler, S., Kerr, J. & Andreotti, V. 2020. Interculturality in teacher education in times of unprecedented global challenges. *Education and Society*, 38(1):13-37. https://doi.org/10.7459/es/38.1.02

Brennan, M. 2017. Struggles for teacher education in the age of the Anthropocene. *Journal of Education*, 69:43-65. Available online: https://bit.ly/3m0UQTe [accessed 14 October 2020].

Cochran-Smith, M., Carney, M.C., Keefe, E.S., Burton, S., Chang, W.C., Fernandez, M.B., Miller, A.F., Sanchez, J.G. & Baker, M. 2018. *Reclaiming accountability in teacher education*. New York: Teachers College Press.

Cochran-Smith, M. & Zeichner, K. 2006. *Studying teacher education*. Washington DC: American Educational Research Association.

Dénommé-Welch, S. & Montero, M. K. 2014. De-colonizing pre-service teacher education: Theatre of the academic absurd. *Journal of Language and Literacy Education*, 10(1):136-165.

De Sousa Santos, B. 2018. *The end of the Cognitive Empire: The coming of age of epistemologies of the south*. Durham: Duke University Press. https://doi.org/10.1215/9781478002000

Freire, P. (1993/1970). *Pedagogy of the Oppressed*. 20th Edition. New York: Continuum.

Furlong, J., Cochran-Smith, M. & Brennan, M. (eds). 2009. *Politics and policy in teacher education: International perspectives*. London: Routledge.

Hayes, D., Mills, M., Christie, P. & Lingard, B. (2006). *Teachers and schooling making a difference: Productive pedagogies, assessment and performance*. Crows Nest: Allen & Unwin.

Kemmis, S. 2009. Understanding professional practice: A synoptic account. In: B. Green (ed.), *Understanding and researching professional practice*. Rotterdam: Sense, pp. 19-38. https://doi.org/10.1163/9789087907327_003

Kemmis, S., Edwards-Groves, C., Lloyd, A., Grootenboer, P., Hardy, I. & Wilkinson, J. 2017. Learning as being 'stirred in' to practices. In: P. Grootenboer, C. Edwards-Groves & S. Choy (eds), *Practice theory perspectives on pedagogy and education: Praxis, diversity and contestation*. Singapore: Springer, pp. 45-65. https://doi.org/10.1007/978-981-10-3130-4_3

Mignolo, W. & Walsh, C. 2018. *On decoloniality: Concepts, analytics, praxis*. Durham, NC: Duke University Press. https://doi.org/10.1215/9780822371779

Smith G.H. & Smith L.T. 2019. Doing indigenous work: Decolonizing and transforming the academy. In: E. McKinley & L. Smith (eds), *Handbook of indigenous education*. Singapore: Springer, pp. 1075-1101. https://doi.org/10.1007/978-981-10-3899-0_69

Soudien, C. 2020. The significance of the decolonial turn in South African higher education. In: T. Oluwaseun & S. Motala (eds), *From ivory towers to ebony towers: Transforming humanities curricula in South Africa, Africa and African-American studies*. Johannesburg: Jacana Media, pp. 33-47.

Tuck, E. & Wang, W.K. 2012. Decolonization is not a metaphor. *Decolonization: Indigeneity, education & society*, 1(1):1-40.

Tyack, D. & Tobin, W. 1994. The 'grammar' of schooling: Why has it been so hard to change? *American Educational Research Journal*, 31(3):453-479. https://doi.org/10.3102/00028312031003453

Wagner, J. 1993. Ignorance in educational research or, how can you *not* know that? *Educational Researcher*, 22:15-23. https://doi.org/10.3102/0013189X022005015

Zeichner, K. 2007. Accumulating knowledge across self-studies in teacher education. *Journal of Teacher Education*, 58(1):36-46. https://doi.org/10.1177/0022487106296219

www.ingramcontent.com/pod-product-compliance
Lightning Source LLC
Chambersburg PA
CBHW081204170426
43197CB00018B/2917